Living Wisely—
For Millennials & Beyond:
Essential Skills to Enhance Life's Journey

Barry M. Cohen, Ph.D.

Learn what life skills are critical for an accomplished life and how to acquire them to jumpstart your journey. A must-read guide for millennials, their parents, and most everyone else.

Copyright © 2018 Barry M. Cohen, Ph.D.

All rights reserved. No part(s) of this book may be reproduced, distributed or transmitted in any form, or by any means, or stored in a database or retrieval systems without prior expressed written permission of the author of this book.

ISBN: 978-1-5356-1541-9

Testimonials

"It takes an honest examination of one's life to truly arrive at wisdom. Barry Cohen has done exactly that in this remarkable compilation of life lessons that offer a path to an enlightened life. In folksy, accessible language, Dr. Cohen draws from his experiences and those of several leaders with whom he has worked to provoke readers to reflect deeply and to practice and learn life skills that lead to a sense of accomplishment and fulfillment. This book has something for everyone, from young adults to seniors."
~ **Regina Romero, Ph.D., Clinical Psychologist and Executive Coach**

"Using a lifetime of professional experience coaching executives as well as his own personal experiences, Barry Cohen has captured the attributes and skills needed to realize personal potential. Most people will likely have some of these skills already, but this book emphasizes their value for readers who might not have thought about them deeply or at all. As a senior executive at several Fortune 100 companies, I have interacted with hundreds of employees at every level. This book will be invaluable in coaching people through their work-related and personal life situations. It is a 'must read' for everyone from older teens to high school counselors to employees in any venture who are looking to become the best they can be. My first thought on reading this book? How helpful it would have been to me when I was in my early twenties." ~ **Geoff Woolford, Ph.D., Biochemistry, Ret. Sr. Officer, Fortune 100 Consumer Products Company**

"Barry Cohen has written a first-rate book filled with valuable information about living well and staying happy. I am eighty-seven years old, and Dr. Cohen's book is helpful to me now and would have been even more helpful when I was seventeen. He covers the waterfront of the attitudes and behaviors that make for a satisfying, fulfilling life. It's a practical, sensible guide. His writing style is direct and conversational. Given the content, this is a surprisingly easy-to-read book. He connects with his readers by a direct, friendly presentation. His personal anecdotes and case histories add credibility and interest to his messages. Even at my age, I felt like a student in Dr. Cohen's class. He is an A+ teacher for old and young minds alike." ~ **Richard J. Smith, Ph.D., Professor Emeritus, University of Wisconsin-Madison, Education Consultant, and Published Author**

"Excellent information for everyone but especially young people seeking personal direction for success. The life examples are very educational and helpful. I would buy this book for my grandchildren and recommend it to my family." ~ **Paul Kudelko, M.D., Retired Cardiologist**

"Reading *Living Wisely*, in many ways, felt as if I was retracing my own life! I personally identified with many of the life lessons. While I agree that chance affects the outcome of one's career, the critical skills highlighted in the book play especially valuable roles. On a personal level, motivation and resilience served me best as I managed investment portfolios through both positive and negative market cycles. Without an abundance of both, I would never have achieved a high level of professional and financial success. I was witness to many failed careers due to a lack of these two skills, no matter how educated or degreed these executives were. This is a book for everyone, young or old, whatever your current position or future direction. It is replete with the good, sound advice that can make a big difference in your life and career." ~ **John Somers, MBA, Retired Senior Officer of TIAA, a Fortune 100 Financial Services Company**

"Reading this book from a perspective of advanced age, I better understand reasons for my successes and failures. If earlier in life I had taken my measure against these life skills markers, some hard knocks would have been avoided. While the greatest benefit from Dr. Cohen's insight will accrue to the young, there is much value here for all ages. Whatever your age, read this book. For the young, those motivated to accomplish something important in life for themselves and their communities and wanting to reduce the uncertainty they feel upon entering adult life, this is the guide for you. From wide personal and professional experience, Dr. Cohen has identified hard-core characteristics of human behavior that lead to an accomplished life. He has travelled the path and has marked a trail to ease the way for others. Here

is advice to replace what in the past have only been vague and sometimes conflicting directions from elders and teachers or what has been left to the individual to learn from bitter experience. Whatever your age, take action! For my part, I will be sending copies of this book to my grandchildren on their coming birthdays!"
~ **Thomas F. Thompson, BEE Electrical Engineer and Retired Senior Officer, Fortune 500 Energy Company**

Acknowledgments

Many people assisted me in the creation of this book. Without their help, this literary work would not have been possible.

I am forever thankful to my editor, Rebecca Chown, who not only meticulously reviewed my every word but also offered many helpful suggestions.

My book reviewers deserve my greatest gratitude. They took time from their busy lives to provide very personal comments. They include Tommy Thompson, Dick Smith, Regina Romero, Paul Kudelko, John Somers, and Geoph Woolford.

I am especially grateful to Ed Northern, an incredible leader and mentor to so many executives I counseled.

My thanks also to Michael Fischer, who read an early version of the book, made edits, and offered helpful suggestions.

I also am thankful to Linda Bialow, who was kind enough to correct my grammar at the very beginning of my writing efforts.

In addition, I want to thank many millennials, including Mitchell Blitzman, Zak Bray, Evan Tiller, Joshua Padilla, and Michael Lerner. Larissa Berendsen, a millennial working parent, contributed unique insights for which I am also very appreciative.

Finally, my dear departed wife, Jewel Cohen, deserves accolades for constantly getting after me to share my wisdoms in a book. I only wish she were here to see what I created.

Contents

Preface: How This Book Was Born 1

Section I: What It Means to "Live Wisely" 5
    Chapter 1: The Secret to Wisdom 7
    Chapter 2: Chance Offers Life Opportunities 11
    Chapter 3: Life Readiness and What Lies Ahead 21

Section II: Life Skills to Acquire As Early As You Can 30
    Chapter 4: Resourcefulness 31
    Chapter 5: Maturity 41
    Chapter 6: Motivation 51

Section III: Life Skills to Cultivate throughout Adulthood 60
    Chapter 7: Leadership 61
    Chapter 8: Active Listening 77
    Chapter 9: Lasting Friendships 87
    Chapter 10: Healthy Romantic Relationships 97
    Chapter 11: Stress Management 109
    Chapter 12: Resilience 119
    Chapter 13: Career Success 137
    Chapter 14: Savvy Financial Habits 153

Section IV: Life Skills to Achieve Your Full Potential 166
    Chapter 15: Happiness 167
    Chapter 16: Smart Aging 175

Chapter 17: Self-Fulfillment and Beyond 187
Inspiration 197
Afterword: Wisdom Takeaways from Millennials 201
Appendix: Select Author Publications 212
About the Author 214

Preface:
How This Book Was Born

THE IDEA FOR THIS BOOK was born in my living room while kidding around with my two precocious grandchildren, who at the time were ages 11 and 14. We were talking about some of my many personal and professional experiences when they put me on the spot by asking why my psychological practice had been limited to helping executives.

They argued that young adults and millennials reaching adulthood in the early twenty-first century needed just as much wisdom and expertise as executives, and they asked if I would write a book chronicling my experiences and insights.

My first thought was that writing such a book would be daunting. Exactly what would I write, and how could I distill my total experience into a clear and practical book illuminating life success? It seemed an overwhelming subject, so I decided to address this unexpected request the same way I tackled other professional projects.

Instead of chronicling all I'd learned in life, I'd approach the task as a psychologist. Thus, I asked myself, "What life skills are critical if young people ages 16 to 30 or thereabouts are to succeed throughout their lives?"

I knew I couldn't come up with a magic formula or brilliant solutions to the vast challenges life presents, but I could come up with those life skills I'd utilized, had observed in my work as an academic psychologist, or had coached others to develop throughout my executive leadership practice.

I also asked myself what life skills were most important for my adolescent grandchildren and others to learn early on. What skills might they profit from the most?

Finally, I asked myself what skills had been of greatest benefit to me over my lifetime now that I was retired and a granddad.

Each chapter in *Living Wisely—For Millennials & Beyond* thus addresses a particular life skill ranging from resourcefulness to maturity to finding love to coping with stress to managing finances to achieving happiness and more. I also include a chapter on smart aging because young people tend to think they'll age gracefully, but medical research shows a wide disparity between individuals who care for their bodies and those who do not. I conclude with the ultimate life skill—self-fulfillment and what lies beyond.

This project took me on an intense journey through the work of other psychologists, life coaches, and medical researchers and through my own personal and professional experiences, including my academic teachings. As I considered various life skills, I deliberately referenced writings available online. Millennials lead hectic lives, and I wanted them to be able to rely on the Internet if they had greater interest in learning more about a particular skill.

Life experience is the basis of all wisdom. I married young, at age 22. I was in love, and life was pure joy. A few years later, just as my academic career was beginning, along came children. I was a husband for 45 years before my wife passed away. I was her caregiver when she had cancer and again when she developed muscular dystrophy. No role I've ever assumed was more trying. Caring for my beloved spouse was a test of love, unconditional giving, and personal sacrifice. Not surprisingly, my roles as father and granddad afforded me many more opportunities to practice wisdoms I learned along life's journey.

Before starting my consulting practice, I spent nearly a decade as a university professor with tenured appointments in both psychology and management at a state university in Florida. I was also licensed as a professional psychologist in the state at that time. As an academic, I taught undergraduates and graduate students, many of whom had families and careers of their own. In addition, as a visiting professor at the MIT Sloan School of Management, I taught doctoral students in industrial and organizational psychology how to assess leadership talents in order to maximize personal success. Essentially, I mentored my students on many of the life skills presented in this book!

After opening my consulting practice as a psychologist and leadership coach, I spent 30 years coaching leaders from different industries in corporate America and in large government agencies to become more impactful while reaching for their full potential personally and professionally. These individuals offered rich examples of life skills they sought to acquire and master. I used my counsel with them as a litmus test for which skills to present in this book.

At age 71 and counting, I chose skills that include examples from my own life and that reflect my expertise as an industrial and organizational psychologist. They also incorporate landmark contributions of other psychologists who added greatly to my knowledge of life success in various fields of human endeavor.

Hence, each life skill reflects three perspectives: my own life experience, my experience as a consulting psychologist with normal healthy populations, and my academic knowledge of the contributions and writings of highly notable psychologists and leading researchers, including a few Nobel Prize winners.

To fully use this book, I encourage readers to hone the skills they need as their lives enfold. Skills needed over a lifetime are presented early in the book. Other skills become more critical in the transitional periods of life throughout adulthood, such as when choosing a career or spouse. Skills needed near the end of life include successfully retiring and achieving a psychological state of well-being and fulfillment.

With the exception of chapter 1, each chapter concludes with a summary of the "life wisdoms" just presented. In addition, each chapter concludes with suggested readings for those who wish to learn more. Most of these recommendations are intended for lay readers, but others are psychological references that corroborate my professional advice and the psychological studies I briefly discuss. In addition, most are from the Internet because millennials increasingly rely on it for learning just about everything they want to know.

Millennials, most especially my grandchildren, I hope you will come back to this book often as you reach different stages in life. Read it when you're a student, perhaps later when you marry and start a family, and then again as your career unfolds.

Finally, someday far in the future, when you retire and perhaps become a grandparent, it would please me a great deal if you would read this book to your grandchildren. Along life's journey, you will surely pick up your own wisdom and add it to mine. Wisdom passed on to future generations is the greatest gift of all.

Section I:

What It Means to "Live Wisely"

Chapter 1:

The Secret to Wisdom

How do people acquire wisdom?

Inevitably, it takes knowledge and experience along with good judgment and intelligence, but even if you're smart, an outstanding expert in your field, and have lived a long and full life, there's still no guarantee you'll acquire wisdom.

The magic ingredient that makes wisdom possible is understanding yourself. If you can explore your life experiences from a variety of perspectives and see how things work and why people behave as they do, you can start to acquire the wisdom necessary to embrace opportunities and tackle life's challenges.

As a 71-year-old grandfather, I've lived a full life with many ups and downs. I've seen a lot happen, pondered what it all meant, and met many different kinds of people. I even counseled quite a few of them. Being married for more than 45 years is also a feat in and of itself. I know exactly how it feels to be a child, adult, husband, parent, and grandparent. Been there, done that!

Wisdom does not simply increase with age but rather increases based on how much you learn from your experiences and those of others. After all, it takes a lot of experience to put things in perspective. Can you do it at an early age? Maybe, but you will surely get better as you acquire more experience. Facing trying life challenges squarely and overcoming them helps develop wisdom over many years of living. Surprisingly, failing a couple of times and getting right back up affords you the opportunity to build what I call "wisdom muscles."

Can using your brain help you acquire wisdom? Yes, but the brain is a very complicated organ. Science has actually shown that three parts of the brain impact wisdom.

At the front of the brain is a large area called the cerebral cortex. This is the seat of all higher order thinking, including how you solve problems and plan ahead, two important components of wisdom.

Two other parts of the brain also contribute to acquiring wisdom, especially in today's complex world. One of them is the limbic system. Located deep in your mid brain, this is the source of feelings such as joy, compassion, and anger. Imagine living without feelings! They are critical for sensing the world and determining how the people around you feel.

Finally, special cells in the brain called mirror neurons help you achieve wisdom, too. These neurons begin firing when you become emotionally involved in something, such as when you watch funny or scary movies. Essentially, they let you "mirror" the feelings you would have if you were literally in those scenes.

Your brain gives you all these tools to read the world around you. As you use your brainpower over your lifetime, you gain wisdom. While the life lessons I share in this book won't impart instant wisdom, they will give you a jumpstart on mastering life's complexities by helping you see things more clearly.

Some of my advice will make immediate sense. When it does, grab it and run. Other concepts will be harder to grasp and might require more life experience on your part.

Don't be surprised if a few ideas don't seem to apply to you. After all, wisdom doesn't come from copying other people. It comes from learning from them and applying what you've learned to better understand yourself.

You are your own unique person. As you read, you will figure out how to benefit from my advice and use what works for you. In the meantime, just remember that wisdom requires you—absolutely requires you—to understand yourself.

Barry M. Cohen, PhD

Recommended Readings

Internet References

Perry, Susan. "Mirror Neurons." *BrainFacts.org*, November 16, 2008. http://www.brainfacts.org/archives/2008/mirror-neurons.

"Scientists 'Discover' Source of Wisdom in the Human Brain." *Daily Mail*, April 5, 2009. http://www.dailymail.co.uk/sciencetech/article-1167633/Scientists-discover-source-wisdom-human-brain.html.

"Wisdom." *Psychology Today*, 2018. https://www.psychologytoday.com/us/basics/wisdom.

"Wisdom." (Scroll to "Psychological Perspectives.") *Wikipedia*, last modified March 31, 2018. https://en.wikipedia.org/wiki/Wisdom, accessed April 9, 2018.

Chapter 2:

Chance Offers Life Opportunities

EVERYTHING IN LIFE HAS A CHANCE of happening. Meteorologists know that better than anyone. They forecast the weather, but they're only right some of the time.

That's life... Sometimes we're right and sometimes we're wrong. Sometimes things work out and sometimes they don't. Everything you do, every decision you make, and every pursuit you embark on has a chance of going well or of not going well.

The miracle of life itself happened by chance, when a unique combination of chemicals combined eons ago and created one-cell creatures so tiny they couldn't have been seen with the naked eye.

Always respect the concept of chance, not only because it created life but because every day, in every way, it affects your well-being and opportunities for success or failure. In fact, because life is about taking chances, it pays to take a moment to assess how you respond when chance opportunities come your way.

Have you ever passed up a valuable opportunity by engaging in any of the following self-defeating behaviors? I'll bet you have. You are human!

- Do you completely miss opportunities because you just can't see good things happening to you? This response reveals pessimistic thinking.

- Do you dismiss opportunities because you tell yourself you're too busy or that your life is already too complicated? This response reveals rationalization.

- Do you fail to see opportunities for what they are because you can't figure out how to make them work in your life? This response reveals limited introspection and personal awareness.

- Do you run from opportunities because you're scared to give them even momentary consideration? This response reveals a low tolerance for risk.

- Do you give opportunities serious thought but then dismiss them because they would force you to make major changes in your life? This response reveals an unwillingness to step out of your comfort zone; it also reveals fear of the unknown.

There are many ways we trick ourselves into not seizing opportunities big and small. All of them are inventions of our own thinking, and they often lead to a great deal of regret later in life.

Take my dad. He lived through the Great Depression and his family struggled a lot. His brother encouraged him to apply to a free city college and said he would even help my dad fill out the application and pay for his books. When the day came to visit the college admissions office to turn in the application, my dad was surprised to find a long line of applicants in front of him. After waiting for what seemed like an interminable time, he gave up and left.

Did my dad not realize how differently his life might have turned out had he earned a college degree? He knew he had the grades to be admitted. Sure enough, years later, he regretted leaving that day. He was determined that his own children would go to college because he wanted more for us than he'd been able to create for himself. Sad as his story is, at least he had the courage to admit his mistake.

Let's say you meet someone, fall deeply in love, and consider getting married. This is a very big decision, one you think will bring you great happiness. But as you might know, almost 50% of all marriages both worldwide and in America end in divorce. This rate drops to around 30% for those who are college educated, marry in their late 20s, and marry someone of the same faith[1]. No one should make this critical life decision without honestly assessing their readiness for partnership and commitment. Interestingly, living together does not improve the odds of a successful marriage[2].

How can you increase your odds of success? Just stepping back and answering this important question can help because it will stop you from making a decision impulsively while giving you valuable time to put your brain muscles—i.e., your wisdom muscles—to work.

Your thinking brain will probably kick in initially. You might analyze the positive qualities that first attracted you to your partner and then everything you learned afterward that made you want to say "I do." However, the emotional parts of your brain will also be going strong. Intense feelings of love and physical attraction might blind you from seeing any negative qualities in this individual. Even if you recognize and accept imperfections, you still need to be fully aware of your emotions before entering marriage.

Feelings affect all life decisions, and they can work for you or against you. Listen to yourself. Step back before making important decisions. A feeling of danger, fear, or hesitation is a signal you should pay attention to, a clue that you should wait and allow your thinking brain to gather more information.

Perhaps you might decide to watch how other people respond to your prospective spouse. Do they enjoy this person? Do their interactions seem

---

1. B.A. Robinson, "Divorce: Encouraging Word; Avoiding Divorce, Personal Story; Conclusion," *Religious Tolerance*, March 20, 2002, http://www.religioustolerance.org/ifm_divo1.htm.

2. "Ten Important Research Findings on Marriage," *For Your Marriage*, 2018, http://www.foryourmarriage.org/blogs/ten-important-research-findings-marriage/.

warm and enthusiastic? Sometimes it's better to observe interactions than to ask for opinions, but take care to pay attention to individuals whose judgment you value. Even if they have a positive opinion of your prospective mate, you cannot escape the fact that making this big decision is entirely up to you.

People face more choices today than ever before in human history, and regrets are par for the course. Princeton University psychologist Daniel Kahneman studied what happens when we have regrets. Kahneman called one kind of regret "hot regret"[3]. It is marked by quick anger at yourself and is short term—you almost want to kick yourself, but the feeling doesn't last forever.

The other type of regret leaves sadness and a bittersweet feeling that life might have turned out very differently if only this or that chance opportunity had been seized. Some individuals regret entering an occupation in their hometown instead of the one that required them to move to a new state. Other people regret turning down the chance to date someone intriguing. Others regret their decision to avoid the class with a reputation for being hard, even though the professor was the best in the whole department. Still others regret staying in a dead-end job instead of putting themselves out there and competing against younger (or smarter or funnier) applicants.

Life consists of a string of large and small decisions. You will sometimes fail, even when the odds of success are high, but you might learn something in the process. You generally have less to lose when you're young, but don't be reckless! The brain isn't fully developed until we reach our mid 20s, but we all make risky decisions far earlier in life. Think of the countless decisions we make every day while driving.

Before taking the wheel, every teenage driver should pause and ask some probing questions. It wouldn't hurt for adults to ask these questions, either. For example, you might ask yourself, "Am I ready to accept this responsibility?

---

3. Sally Squires, "The Road Not Taken Is the One We Regret," *Los Angeles Times*, January 8, 1995, http://articles.latimes.com/1995-01-08/news/ls-17507_1_long-term.

How careful am I? Do I lose my cool easily? Am I easily distracted, or can I maintain my concentration for a long time?"

By asking thoughtful questions and answering them honestly, you can assess your potential to be a good driver even before you learn to drive. Now that is the beginning of wisdom, and this approach can be applied to every decision you make.

If life is filled with risks that can cause us to fail, it is also full of opportunities that allow us to succeed. The song says, "Don't worry; be happy," but that's easier said than done. The brain has a built-in risk aversion or "avoidance system" that helped in primitive times when sheer survival was on the line. The remnants of that system remain today. Hence, some fear is good, even if it doesn't always feel that way, because it can keep you alert, push you to perform at a higher level, and keep you vigilant and thoughtful when chance opportunities come along. In my opinion, the song might better be phrased, "Worry and be happy; just be careful and do your best."

But fear can also get the best of you. It can slow you down, cause you to lose concentration, and even cause you to lose valuable sleep. When fear is chronic, it can be exhausting. Entertainers sometimes get so uptight, so filled with what's called stage fright, that they can't perform. What can be done about this?

To conquer fear, you must face it, sometimes several times. Doing so might surprise you. The fear might not be nearly as bad as you imagined, in part because fear tends to exaggerate itself.

When fear gets to you, ask yourself, "What's the worst thing that can happen?"

Then ask yourself, "If I give it my best effort, what can I accomplish?"

By weighing the worst possible outcomes against the best, you let your thinking brain step in and help you decide what to do.

Few of us press ourselves to the maximum. If you get there, I applaud you, but I strongly advise you to press yourself to go further, until you fail. Yes, until you fail, because that's how you discover your true potential. Failure is a natural part of living fully.

Psychologists practicing in industry often coach talented employees to reach for their full potential and to discover their hidden talents. Of course, other employees can sometimes see talents that coworkers and colleagues fail to see in themselves.

In my practice, I sometimes tried to use feedback to whack an underperforming person on the side of the head. You would be surprised at how many people underestimate their own strengths, and you would also be surprised at the reasons this is so.

Discovering our own hidden talents is complicated. Taking chances is worrisome. We need to push ourselves in order to realize what we can do, but most of the time, we seek out comfort zones instead. Here is a very unique way that companies are beginning to press employees beyond familiar boundaries in a way that requires these employees to take chances.

Imagine you've been assigned to a new project with a team of individuals from different parts of your company and various areas of expertise. Your team of strangers is asked to come up with a plan to introduce a new product in an entirely new market. The team is encouraged to seek out leading experts for advice, but the actual work must be done by the team. Finally, team members must share their ideas with the CEO of the company in a formal presentation followed by a demanding question-and-answer discussion.

This is a great although challenging way to discover your hidden talents even while the company greatly benefits from your work. This kind of leadership development is called "action learning." The psychological principles of such learning come from the work of the great education professor Dr. Malcolm Knowles, who understood that taking chances was an essential part of learning and accomplishment[4].

Of course, the healthier you keep yourself physically and mentally, the greater the likelihood you can succeed when chance opportunities come

---

4. Christopher Pappas, "The Adult Learning Theory–Andragogy–Malcolm Knowles," *eLearning Industry*, May 9, 2013, https://elearningindustry.com/the-adult-learning-theory-andragogy-of-malcolm-knowles.

your way. I don't mean just not getting sick; I mean eating well, exercising regularly, developing close friendships, and enjoying yourself. Your body, your emotions, and your thoughts are all interconnected. They can prepare you to face tough challenges in life.

In sum, here are my life wisdoms regarding chance opportunities:

- All events in life have a chance of happening. The miracle of life was a great chance happening. Other events just happen and there's nothing anyone can do about them. People are injured or killed all the time because they were in the wrong place at the wrong time. Chance isn't good or bad… It's both. Such is life.

- How do you respond when chance opportunities come your way? Is this a healthy response, or are you tricking yourself into overlooking opportunities that could greatly enrich your life?

- Pause before making really big decisions and find out the odds of success or failure. You can find statistics for just about every important decision in life. Just look at the stats in Major League Baseball. Managers use them all the time before making game plays.

- Don't let high odds of failure stop you. People get married all the time despite the risky odds. Baseball players know the odds are low they'll make it to the major leagues. That doesn't stop them from going for it. Just know your odds before trying and compare what you might gain with what you might lose before you seize the courage to go for it, whatever "it" might be.

- Use your brainpower when making risky decisions. Gather as many facts as you can. Observe other people and ask for their opinions. Pay close attention to your feelings. If they're troubling, you're either not ready to make a decision or you're actually deciding against something; you just haven't acknowledged it yet. Step away to analyze the opportunity further or redefine your decision in a fresh way. Sometimes experience is the best teacher, especially if it helps you gain new insights about yourself. Remember, understanding yourself is the magical ingredient of wisdom, so size yourself up before making important decisions. Honestly examine yourself and ask probing questions to assess your likelihood of success.

- Fear is natural. It can lead you to do great things you might not otherwise believe you could do. Fear can also stop you from trying. To perform at your best, you need a certain amount of fear to sharpen your senses and attention. The better your physical and mental health, the better prepared you will be to reach beyond what you thought you could do.

- Put yourself in demanding situations that will lead you to great discoveries about your talents, including some you might not even realize you have. Cutting-edge companies are using this principle more and more to develop future leaders. If you have the opportunity to take such a chance, count yourself fortunate.

- Remember to worry, be happy, be careful, and do your best, no matter what chance opportunities come your way!

Recommended Readings

Internet References

National Institute of Mental Health. "The Teen Brain: Still Under Construction." Accessed April 11, 2018. https://infocenter.nimh.nih.gov/pubstatic/NIH%2011-4929/NIH%2011-4929.pdf.

Pappas, Christopher. "The Adult Learning Theory–Andragogy–Malcolm Knowles." *eLearning Industry*, May 9, 2013. https://elearningindustry.com/the-adult-learning-theory-andragogy-of-malcolm-knowles.

Robinson, B.A. "Divorce: Encouraging Word; Avoiding Divorce, Personal Story; Conclusion." *Religious Tolerance*, March 20, 2002. http://www.religioustolerance.org/ifm_divo1.htm.

Soleil, Gina. "The Secret to Conquering Fear in Business." *Huffington Post*, January 22, 2016. https://www.huffingtonpost.com/gina-soleil-/the-secret-to-conquering-_b_9039738.html.

Squires, Sally. "The Road Not Taken Is the One We Regret." *Los Angeles Times*, January 8, 1995. http://articles.latimes.com/1995-01-08/news/ls-17507_1_long-term.

"Ten Important Research Findings on Marriage." *For Your Marriage*, 2018. http://www.foryourmarriage.org/blogs/ten-important-research-findings-marriage/.

Than, Ker. "How Did Life Arise on Earth?" *Live Science*, September 1, 2016. https://www.livescience.com/1804-greatest-mysteries-life-arise-earth.html.

Chapter 3:

Life Readiness and What Lies Ahead

Your journey through life will be unique. You will take both planned and unexpected turns. No one can fully anticipate the many challenges and exciting opportunities that lie ahead, but as you acquire wisdom about yourself, you will make some very personal decisions, among them:

- Am I ready to attend college or a university?
- Am I ready to get married or embark on a committed life-long relationship?
- Am I ready to become a parent and raise children?
- Am I prepared to support my family and/or myself financially?
- Am I ready to retire, give up my life's work, and launch my retirement?

These are very critical life-readiness questions. Answering them will require you to step back and assess your ability and enthusiasm to assume roles and responsibilities that will demand a great deal from you. As you learn more about yourself, you will hopefully make these decisions with great care. Even then, life comes with no guarantees. You will step into unknown territory, but that's okay because life is about taking chances. What might be coming your way?

The youngest millennials must decide whether or not to attend college. If you're one of them, think about what personal qualities you'll need for college success. The triumphs you've enjoyed in high school should give you a good idea of your study habits and the subjects you most enjoy. In other words, your high school grades will partially predict your likelihood of college success. Universities use your grades as one important criterion for admission. Most also use aptitude tests to predict how well you'll handle the academic challenges that lie ahead.

However, even if you "pass" these hurdles and are accepted to a college or university, you aren't necessarily ready to attend and succeed. Some very smart people drop out for personal or financial reasons. This is something I observed many times early in my career as a university professor.

Once you've been admitted to a college or university, you will need to step back and determine if this is the right decision for you at this time in your life. It takes personal discipline to successfully pursue college studies. Your professors won't keep after you. Some courses will interest you, but others will feel like drudgery. Are you the kind of student who can stick with things even if they don't appeal to you? Are you an achiever? Do accomplishments matter to you at this juncture of your life, or will you aimlessly drift along in the hopes of "discovering" yourself?

If you're ambivalent or unsure about your commitment, you might be better off taking a few night courses at a community college before becoming a full-time student. You can earn college credits while deciding whether you want to get serious about earning a college degree. In the meantime, you can save money and get some work experience.

While financial aid is available, many college graduates find themselves saddled with large student loans. This is a national problem and also a personal one, because borrowing a great deal of money to go to college causes significant challenges. The good news is, community colleges and state universities are less expensive than private schools, and many are outstanding. Some states offer stipends or "free money" for attending college, and every penny helps! I lived at home and attended an outstanding city college for free, and I'm glad I did. As a result, I had more money to help pay for graduate school. After graduate school, I got a fellowship to pursue my doctoral training that came with free tuition and expense money.

It takes a lot of financial savvy to determine the best way to finance your education, especially if you expect to pursue an advanced degree or degrees after your four years of undergraduate work. Just remember, it's not wise to overextend yourself and take on a lot of debt in college.

Remember, too, that life starts to get complicated when you attend college. Not only must you keep up with your grades and pay tuition, but you must also adjust to college life, which is a challenge in and of itself. You will probably want to date and make new friends. I was lucky enough to meet the girl I eventually married when I was in college, but know in advance that there is more than one special someone out there for those who are looking for a soul mate.

In hindsight, I didn't go about dating with any measure of mature thought. I once met two college women visiting Florida on spring break. As we chatted, I casually asked about their preferences in a mate. One said she was looking for someone who enjoyed the music she liked! She clearly wasn't focused on finding the best possible person; she just wanted to have fun.

The other woman was studying accounting and seriously looking for "Mr. Special," as she put it. She wanted a best friend she could respect and trust to be loyal and responsible. In my opinion, she was much better prepared for a committed relationship because she was looking for a guy who was right for her.

Of course, falling in love is something most people yearn for, but it takes a lot more than love to make a relationship work over the long haul. After you've dated for a while, I encourage you to describe to yourself the kind of person who might be best for you. You won't know for sure, but at least this exercise will give you some serious food for thought.

Nowadays, people get married later in life. You'll likely find someone special when you're in your late twenties or even your thirties. By then, young people have much more knowledge about who they are and what they want in a committed relationship. Getting married young is riskier, but that doesn't mean it can't work out. If Cupid strikes early in college, I hope you will still date other people. After all, this is one of the most important decisions you will make in your entire life.

Once you find your special someone, assuming your career is progressing, you might want to consider raising a family. Bear in mind that children aren't right for everyone and that raising even one child is a huge financial commitment. It takes about a quarter of a million dollars to raise a child until the age of 18, and many parents help financially way past that age[5]. Having children is a great responsibility, and there's no turning back once they're born. They will depend on you for love, care, guidance, learning, and all kinds of emotional support.

Do you love children? Do you have the maturity to raise a child, or do you want independence and freedom? There is no shame in not having children. Parents who ignore their children or busily pursue their careers at the expense of their families are asking for trouble. Kids need affection and love above all else.

Of course, two-career families, single-parent families, and adopted families can all work, too. Successful parents find ways to make their families thrive, but above all, unconditional love is the magic ingredient in parenting. Generational researchers have found that young adults today value parenthood and family more than past generations. In fact, they value parenthood even more than career success.

It's inevitable that when a family member dies or parents break up, families are thrown into turmoil. Divorce can be a huge blow, especially if it's fraught with conflict and anger. If ever there was a time when best friends were important, this is it. Stress takes a great toll on everyone. To get past it is far from easy, especially when financial burdens add additional pressure. While there's no way to avoid the pain, parents in turmoil need to emotionally and physically care for themselves. If they don't, their children

---

5. Kathryn Vasel, "It Costs $233,610 to Raise a Child," *CNN*, January 9, 2017, http://money.cnn.com/2017/01/09/pf/cost-of-raising-a-child-2015/index.html.

suffer even more. Support groups and family counselors can be of great benefit at these times of crisis.

Families are also deeply stressed when a partner loses a job. Many families live close to the edge financially. They often don't have savings or a financial cushion for unexpected emergencies. Some don't have medical insurance, and most have no disability insurance. When I was in my late thirties, I decided to drop our family medical plan for a cheaper one with a $10,000 deductible clause. That meant the insurance company only covered our expenses once we'd reached $10,000 in costs per year. I liked this policy because everyone in my family was healthy and no one ever needed hospitalization, but when my wife learned about my decision, she said I was playing with fire. I decided she was right and chose a medical policy with even more coverage than the previous policy.

One year later, my wife became very sick with ovarian cancer. Our hospital bills totaled almost one and a half million dollars! Our family would have faced a huge financial setback had I kept the inexpensive policy. Fortunately, my wife knew better, and I listened to her. Never play Russian roulette with your family's welfare.

Unless you learn how to save money and develop the discipline to do so, financial strain can take a big toll. I have never lived at the peak of what I could afford. Even as a kid, when I received a small sum of money each week for my allowance, I tried very hard not to ask my dad for any more money because I knew he couldn't afford it. Even after my career took off and I began earning money, I didn't buy a lavish home. I preferred a comfortable home, and eventually I paid off the mortgage. Debt of any kind can strangle you. Credit card debt is the worst kind because interest rates are so high. Make it a lifelong habit to pay your credit cards off in full each month. If you can't do this, you are living beyond your means, which means it's time to cut back on your spending!

Once you're debt free, you can save a lot of money. There are many ways to do so. For one thing, you can buy municipal bonds that yield tax-free interest. You should also start a Roth IRA as soon as possible. Investments of this kind accumulate tax-free for your lifetime. If you don't spend the money, your kids can inherit it entirely tax-free! These strategies build wealth and help you achieve financial independence. They can also cushion the blow if you need cash in an emergency.

If all goes well, someday you will think about retiring. If you've saved wisely and enjoyed a successful career, you might have the opportunity to retire early. Should you do so or wait until later? If you retire now, what will you do with the rest of your life?

Typically, the first question individuals ask themselves as they think about retirement is, "How much money will I need?" However, readiness to retire also takes a great deal of psychological adjustment. Issues that might need to be addressed include loss of career identity, the need to replace support networks at work, the pros and cons of spending more time with your spouse, and developing an active lifestyle of leisure pursuits.

Psychologist Robert Delamontagne found that while some people make this important life transition smoothly, others experience anxiety, depression, and debilitating feelings of loss when they retire[6]. Some of these individuals even go through hell but never say a word about it because they're embarrassed. After all, our culture teaches us that retirement is all about finally living "the good life."

A 2012 study of recent retirees found that many experienced a "sugar rush" of happiness shortly after they retired followed by a steep decline in happiness a few years later[7]. Why? Because retirement requires you to recreate your life, and that means relying on a great deal of self-understanding about what makes you happy.

If ever you needed to draw on wisdom, now's the time! It all comes down to what you want. I've known workaholics who just couldn't retire. They felt

---

6. Jamie Chamberlin, "Retiring Minds Want to Know," *American Psychological Association*, 45, no. 1 (January 2014): 61, http://www.apa.org/monitor/2014/01/retiring-minds.aspx.

7. Ibid.

compelled to work for reasons other than financial necessity. If you're one of them, your only choice is to continue working as long as you can. You can cut back gradually, but make it your choice. In the meantime, you can lead a blended life of work and leisure well into your retirement years.

If for some reason you're a workaholic who is forced to retire, get another job or two. You might discover a variation on your career that you enjoy even more than the work you just retired from. For example, a dermatologist might leave a busy medical practice to take part ownership of a small hospital specializing in treating burn patients or join a company selling specialty surgical dermatology supplies.

If you've led a balanced life and found time for your family, your leisure pursuits, and your community, you're a good candidate for retirement. In other words, you already have other interests and no doubt want to pursue them further. In all likelihood, you will be incredibly happy in retirement. Some people gain expertise and knowledge in areas very different than their chosen careers, discover entirely new life purposes, or even reinvent themselves. My hat is off to them!

I thought I wanted to travel around the world after I retired, but my career included a great deal of travel that I found taxing. I do travel a lot today, but long trips aren't nearly as much fun as visiting old friends and seeing new places both near and far.

My retirement is a product in creation along my life's journey. For me, successful retirement includes growing and learning personally, making new friends, and enjoying myself. Right now, I'm also writing books. It's great fun and also a process of self-discovery.

What's next?

Who knows. That's what makes retirement so interesting.

In sum, here are my life-readiness wisdoms:

- All of life is a journey, and it's up to you to assess your readiness to enter different life-changing roles along the way. Ask yourself, "Am I willing and able to accept these new responsibilities?" While chance plays a part, insight and forethought can guide your life choices and increase your odds of success.

- Attending college requires adjustments. It takes self-discipline, good study habits, and the ability to cope with the many demands of academic life. Be careful not to take on too much debt!

- There is more than one special soul mate out there for those who want a serious committed relationship. Dating a lot of people will help you sort out who and what you want. Take the time to do this. We all have different needs. Know what you want *and* need in a successful relationship.

- Having a family is a critical personal and financial decision. No one can live on love alone. Don't get caught in the trap of taking on significant debt. Scrimp and save while you're young. Set realistic savings goals and learn how to invest wisely. If you want children, know in advance they aren't cheap. Families that live on the financial edge endure a lot of stress.

- Retirement isn't for everyone. If you're a workaholic, retiring is the worst decision you can make. Better to try new jobs that are rewarding and/or launch a second or third career. If you've led a balanced life, retirement might indeed afford you great opportunities to grow personally. Either way, with a little imagination and resourcefulness, your retirement can bring you great joy.

Recommended Readings

Internet References

Chamberlin, Jamie. "Retiring Minds Want to Know." *American Psychological Association*, 45, no. 1 (January 2014): 61. http://www.apa.org/monitor/2014/01/retiring-minds.aspx.

"Five Saving Strategies." *America Saves*, 2017. https://americasaves.org/for-savers/make-a-plan-how-to-save-money/five-strategies-to-saving.

Killinger, Barbara. "The Workaholic Breakdown Syndrome—Loss of Communication Skills." *Psychology Today*, August 9, 2012. https://www.psychologytoday.com/us/blog/the-workaholics/201208/the-workaholic-breakdown-syndrome-loss-communication-skills.

Sightings, Tom. "8 Differences between Boomers and Millennials." *U.S. News*, May 20, 2014. https://money.usnews.com/money/blogs/on-retirement/2014/05/20/8-differences-between-boomers-and-millennials.

Vasel, Kathryn. "It Costs $233,610 to Raise a Child." *CNN*, January 9, 2017. http://money.cnn.com/2017/01/09/pf/cost-of-raising-a-child-2015/index.html.

SECTION II:

Life Skills to Acquire As Early As You Can

Chapter 4:

Resourcefulness

RESOURCEFULNESS IS AN INCREDIBLY useful quality. If you can develop any single life skill to the maximum in your lifetime, make this the one. If you can be resourceful when the going gets tough, you'll be fine no matter what comes your way. You'll even be an effective decision maker in the face of inadequate information. Instead of wallowing in wonder, you'll look online, call an authority, or talk to someone who's already been there, done that in order to position yourself to act.

A former company client defined resourcefulness as "out-of-the-box thinking," a term that spread like wildfire throughout corporate America and into everyday life.

Here are a few times in life when you might benefit from out-of-the-box thinking:

- When you want to make a decision but are stumped, with no idea of what to do

- When you're up against the wall and still need to do something

- When you're trying to figure something out but keep running into the proverbial brick wall

- When other people want you to conform or do what they do, but you want to take your own unique path, even though it's never been tried before

- When you wish you could invent something new but find yourself on the proverbial treadmill, doing the same thing over and over

- When you have fleeting or incomplete thoughts and are close to a breakthrough but can't quite put everything together

Business training seminars can help people develop resourcefulness, especially in fields that require workers to make entirely new products, use existing products in new ways, or come up with clever and fresh business solutions, but here's the catch: *individuals vary markedly in their ability to be resourceful even after they've been trained.*

However useful, resourcefulness is a complicated and uncommon human quality. Why can't everyone figure out how to be resourceful? Before I attempt to answer this question, let me explain my perspective on resourcefulness by explaining how to make what I call "Resourcefulness Soup."

Ingredients needed for Resourcefulness Soup include the following:

- Two teaspoons of intelligence—use your smarts

- Two teaspoons of imaginative thinking—invent items or ideas that don't exist now

- Three teaspoons of playfulness—have fun letting yourself enjoy something just for the sake of enjoying it

- Four teaspoons of tenacity—don't give up, no matter how frustrated you get

- Five teaspoons of possibility thinking—get past conventional thinking to see new possibilities

- Five teaspoons of mental flexibility—look at things from entirely new vantage points that go beyond how others think

Combine these ingredients, and you've got a rich and satisfying broth that will nourish your ability to handle any challenge that comes your way.

Now, to answer the question of why people struggle to learn how to be resourceful. It's because they need all these ingredients to do it well! Even when they have all the ingredients, they still need to recognize the best opportunities to use or apply them.

I encourage you to assess yourself now and at different stages of your life using the recipe for Resourcefulness Soup. Remember, wisdom requires self-examination. Just don't be surprised if you have difficulty judging yourself, especially if you're very young. It's tough to realistically assess your resourcefulness until you're an adult because only then do you have the wide range of experiences you need to fully know yourself.

You might assume playfulness is one ingredient you have in abundance, but that's probably not the case. Playfulness is actually far more common in children than adults. Preschoolers play a game called "make believe" that helps their brains develop, but as we grow into adulthood, we often forget to be playful. Sometimes we're even discouraged from using our imaginations. By the time we're adults and ready to embark on a career, most of us have forgotten how to be playful. Please don't let that happen to you!

Remember when you first played with a hula hoop? Think about that interesting product for a moment. All the inventor of the hula hoop did was think of a new way to use plastic. This individual was resourceful, and so was the creator of the wonderfully helpful Post-it Notes, who thought entirely out of the box in order to find a use for his accidental creation of a very weak adhesive. When you're playful, you come up with entirely fresh ways of doing or making things. Life regularly presents new possibilities if you can be mentally flexible enough to see them.

Want some practical ideas to help you incorporate resourcefulness into your daily life? Here are some ideas from a seasoned trainer[8]:

- Don't reinvent the wheel. Seek clever solutions that others have already shared with the world. For example, want to learn to juggle? Get the book *Juggling for the Complete Klutz*. Benefit from the mistakes others have already made and the hard-earned knowledge that's out there for the taking.
- Learn everything you can about *how* to be a smart information seeker. For example, make it a habit to use the Internet, but expand the search by checking out the local library.
- Make necessity work for you. For example, if you want to attend a sold-out concert, get clever and persistent by searching high and wide. Get the word out to your friends and relatives, use third-party Internet vendors, Facebook your friends, or go to the concert early and solicit tickets from people who might have an extra ticket or two.

Some of my own life experiences reveal how resourcefulness affected or improved my life:

- I recently bought an iPhone and asked the vendor to put my home telephone number and name on the phone in case I lost it. My teenage grandson quickly wrote my identifying information on a piece of paper, took a picture of the paper with my iPhone, and transferred it to my iPhone's home screen. There it is, every time anyone turns on my phone.
- When I was a college freshman, I took integral and differential calculus taught by a new professor who was difficult to understand. Soon, most of the class was failing, and I was struggling to earn even

---

8. Lorie Marrero, "How to Promote Resourcefulness in Yourself and Others," *Lifehack*, https://www.lifehack.org/articles/featured/how-to-promote-resourcefulness-in-yourself-and-others.html.

a "C." At the final exam, worth 40% of our grade, every student in class was sweating. I managed to answer most of the problems and thought I might pass, but when I read the last problem, I knew I couldn't solve it if my life depended on it. With time running out, I decided to write out my approach to solving the problem. I was desperate and resourceful. The professor appreciated my efforts, and I passed the course with a "C."

- When I was a senior in college, I needed a part-time job to help earn money to pay my tuition in graduate school. The highest-paying jobs were at the World's Fair in New York City close to my home. Once I'd landed a job cleaning toilets at minimum wage, I had one foot in the door! Then I visited a restaurant doing a thriving business at one of the pavilions. Customers were lined up out the door, eager to buy one of the restaurant's inexpensive steak dinners. I spoke to the flustered and extremely busy manager about a job and soon learned the only job available was cashier. He desperately needed someone, but this person had to have experience using his machines. I had no experience as a cashier, but I was resourceful. I told the manager I'd handled cash at a restaurant before. He was so busy that he immediately put me to work. I thought, "What do I do now?" and quickly asked my fellow cashier for help. I explained that I'd used a cash register before (yes, a white lie), just not this model. My co-worker taught me how to use it, and I managed to get through the day with my high-paying job intact. Resourceful thinking literally paid off, and I earned enough to pay for my first semester in graduate school!

- My cashiering experience led to still another opportunity to be resourceful. Within a week, I'd mastered my job, but my boss said the number of meals I rang up didn't equal the cash in my drawer and that I had too much money left in my register at the end of the week. I was intrigued, and then it hit me. I gave my customers bills in change for their purchases, but they often left their change behind because they forgot to look for it coming out of the slot return on the register. I decided to redefine this problem as an opportunity. I began checking the change slot after every transaction, and if any coins were left behind, I closed my register down and ran after those customers. Much to my delight, many of them told me to "keep the change" as a tip for running after them. When I couldn't chase them down, I just deposited those coins in my college fund. I had no choice, because my boss said he'd fire me if I continued to have overruns. After my second week, my boss was raving about my work. My register balanced almost perfectly, and what's more, many customers personally commended me for helping them. At the end of the summer, my boss asked me to manage one of his restaurants. I was flattered, but I turned the job down because I was about to start graduate school.

- When I was 10 years old, I attended a local carnival with one dime in my pocket. I saw adults betting coins as a wheel turned and a winning number came up, and I slipped between them and put my dime on a bet paying 25 to 1. Now that's taking a chance, especially since I had no business placing a bet in the first place, but I ended up winning $2.50. That would be the equivalent of about $15.00 today. Instead of buying a toy or candy with the money, I used the cash to pay the fare to go out on an all-day fishing boat. I had no idea the boat would take me all the way out to beautiful Long Island Sound! There, I saw incredibly beautiful homes on the shoreline set off by swimming pools and lavishly landscaped backyards. I was a city kid growing up surrounded by apartment buildings and cement. Right then and there, I promised myself I'd live in a beautiful waterfront home someday. Sure enough, I made that dream come true.

Resourcefulness requires thinking outside the box. Happily, it can be taught and learned. Resourceful individuals might be rare, but that doesn't mean you can't be one of them. Sian Beilock[9], a psychologist at the University of Chicago, offers the following mental "tricks" to help people think in fresh and unexpected ways to solve problems that stump them cold:

- Take a break from brainstorming a difficult problem. Get up from your desk, take a walk outdoors, even take a relaxing bath. This allows your brain to work in the background, piecing together fragments of information about the problem that have been swirling around in your thoughts. Legend has it that Archimedes coined the term "eureka" when he discovered the principles of buoyancy while soaking in his tub!

- Try sketching or drawing the problem on paper. For example, if you need to cut your department's budget, instead of detailing the numbers, start with an organizational chart showing each job and its function. This can help you see redundancies or even positions that can be merged or eliminated. Our brains sometimes do better thinking in pictures than by analyzing numbers and facts.

- Turn off your brain. I have found that my most inventive thinking occurs during the middle of the night. If I awaken then and think of my problem, imaginative solutions often start pouring in.

- Distance yourself from the problem. Put it entirely out of your mind and forget about it. If possible, do this for several days. Psychologists call this "creating psychological distance," and studies show that it works. The brain needs time to incubate problems, and individuals are often able to subconsciously devise effective solutions without even being aware that it's happening.

As I've said, the brain is an incredible organ and is quite capable of generating remarkable solutions. Sometimes we just need to prime it in

---

9. Caitlin Carlson, "Five Creative Ways to Solve Any Problem," *Women's Health*, September 11, 2013, https://www.womenshealthmag.com/life/problem-solving.

order to get the most out of it. In sum, here are my wisdoms about being resourceful:

- Resourcefulness means thinking differently from most people. It all starts with being playful as a child. Most adults aren't nearly as playful as kids. Find ways to enjoy play all your life. If you have kids, join in their play. Don't just watch them!

- When problems arise and you don't know what to do, reframe them as challenges, look at them from different perspectives, and invent new ways of solving them. Sometimes solutions are right in front of your face.

- Don't go through life merely analyzing things. Practice using your imagination or you will lose the ability to do so. Imagination is a muscle that can take you far, but if it isn't used, it will lie dormant or even wither. Sometimes it's better to think of possibilities than probabilities. Be curious and inventive. This is how you add richness to life. You might hit upon a big money-making idea or even a way to change many lives for the better.

- Cultivate the ingredients you need to make Resourcefulness Soup. It's delicious!

- Resourcefulness needs to be examined and reexamined at different stages of life. With new experiences, diverse jobs, new acquaintances, and a little determination, your ability to use this incredible life skill will change for the better.

Recommended Readings

Internet References

Baldoni, John. "Wanted: Resourceful People to Change Your World." *Forbes*, December 10, 2012. https://www.forbes.com/sites/

johnbaldoni/2012/12/10/four-ways-to-teach-your-employees-to-be-resourceful/#20b1b0554cf8.

Carlson, Caitlin. "Five Creative Ways to Solve Any Problem." *Womens Health*, September 11, 2013. https://www.womenshealthmag.com/life/problem-solving.

"Ingenuity," *Wikipedia*, last modified September 17, 2017. https://en.wikipedia.org/w/index.php?title=Ingenuity&oldid=801112406, accessed April 9, 2018.

Marrero, Lorie. "How to Promote Resourcefulness in Yourself and Others." *Lifehack*. https://www.lifehack.org/articles/featured/how-to-promote-resourcefulness-in-yourself-and-others.html.

Murphy, Bill, Jr. "7 Things Really Resourceful People Do." *Inc.*, March 28, 2014. https://www.inc.com/bill-murphy-jr/7-things-really-resourceful-people-do.html.

Wax, Dustin. "11 Ways to Think Outside the Box." *Lifehack*. https://www.lifehack.org/articles/featured/11-ways-to-think-outside-the-box.html.

"Why You Should Have a Child-Like Imagination (and the Research That Proves It)." *Ideas to Go*, June 2, 1017. https://www.ideastogo.com/articles-on-innovation/why-you-should-have-a-child-like-imagination-and-the-research-that-proves-it.

Chapter 5:

Maturity

I SOMETIMES ASK ADULTS how mature they think they are. The healthier individuals either say they've done dumb things in their lives but have learned from these experiences or tell me they're getting more mature all the time.

By contrast, individuals who struggle to answer my question or blithely claim they are indeed mature generally have little self-awareness.

What is "maturity?" Psychologists agree that maturity is the ability to make the most of life, but how is that accomplished? There's no simple answer. If you look up the word "mature," you learn that it's an attempt to advance toward perfection. However, this is a quality no one can ever quite reach, which means maturity is a journey in pursuit of making life as fulfilling as possible.

If this sounds complex, it is! People in tune with themselves appreciate that maturity is about personal learning and isn't something they can master in a lifetime. There's always more to learn, and many note that their biggest mistakes offered them their greatest opportunities.

The easiest and most powerful way to learn about yourself is to recognize your strengths and find clever ways to capitalize on them. Don't take your strengths for granted. That isn't a sign of maturity. Accomplished people learn to capitalize on their talents in new and different ways.

For example, if you're a great listener, use this skill to help a distraught friend, make new friends, become a talented leader, or add value to a team, sports or otherwise. Mature people are always looking for different ways to apply their strengths to life; they deliberately search for new opportunities to do this.

Immature people stumble on opportunities to use their strengths. When these strengths result in success, even extraordinary success, they pass it off as "just luck" or, worse yet, dismiss it as "no big deal." Psychologists call such reactions "self-sealing" because they inhibit mature learning.

Never ignore your talents! You don't have to brag about them, but if you're blessed with talents, you owe it to yourself to use them to improve your life.

The great philosopher Socrates was famous for saying, "Know thyself." There are several ways to get to know yourself; each individual has to find what works for them. Asking for personal feedback from people who know you well and whom you respect can net invaluable insights, but always weigh the source of the feedback you receive. Sometimes it's vague and opinionated, and sometimes it's given in the heat of anger or haste. Even so, mature people are open to feedback even when it's disagreeable and hard to hear.

Feedback is a gift. Gems are often buried within feedback, even feedback that is otherwise inaccurate and more a personal reflection of the other person than it is of you!

Also be aware that some people see negative qualities in others that they can't or don't want to see in themselves. It's a way of ignoring what we find threatening. Even so, it doesn't mean that feedback from these individuals is entirely untrue. Learn everything you can about yourself, even if it isn't all flattering. Your listening will improve, too!

The following life experiences—i.e., opportunities—highlight five common ways to learn more about yourself and to become more mature.

1. Embark on a personal growth program. Learning programs abound. Topics run the gamut from communication skills to interpersonal sensitivity to conflict resolution. My wife and I once attended a professional training session together. Her group consisted of a psychiatrist from South America, a medical director of a large university clinic, a couple from the

Irish Republican Army, the director of admissions of a large university, and two school educators.

My wife's job was to give straightforward and unvarnished feedback to those in her group, which earned her the moniker "The Hammer." Ever after, she tried utilizing this concept of giving constructive feedback. Sometimes it worked and sometimes it didn't, but it became a lifetime learning pursuit, and that in itself is a sign of maturity.

2. Make tough life decisions. When you're at a crossroads and facing a decision that will send you down one path or another, you have to take stock of yourself in new ways. When I finished graduate school, I entertained diverse job offers. One job was in Manhattan working for a huge retail company where I would have free rein to use my talents under the supervision of a gifted psychologist.

The decision was anguishing, but I turned this job down for one that paid about half as much at a university just starting up in Florida where I could join the faculty and teach at the graduate school.

The corporate job offered financial security and significant professional development, but the academic position offered a great climate near the beautiful Gulf of Mexico. I had a young family, and my wife and I felt that quality of life was a top priority. I also was excited to design a new graduate program and train students in my field.

In hindsight, my university experience combined with local consulting work was ideal preparation for eventually starting my own consulting practice with large global companies. Nonetheless, when I first decided to join the university, I had no idea how my career would advance. That awareness didn't come until years later.

Of course, making tough life decisions of necessity involves saying no, whether to an individual or to an opportunity. Though it can be difficult, there's power in saying no. Even when the decision is stressful, those who say no have the satisfaction of knowing they're steering their own ships. It can be surprisingly difficult to say no to tempting commitments, especially at work, but those who can't manage this, at least on occasion, lose control of their lives.

3. Discover your own natural talents. I was once asked what "natural talent" is. I explained that it's something you do extraordinarily well without much thought. It comes easily and is just a knack you have. In sports, a baseball player might have an uncanny ability to spot a pitch right out of the pitcher's hand or a baseball fielder might have a knack for judging exactly where a ball might go after it's hit. These two natural talents are acute perception and rapid reaction time. If coached to use their gifts in batting or fielding, these two guys could become great players. In other words, becoming aware of how to capitalize on a natural talent is a formula for success.

One of my natural talents is the ability to meet people and get them to comfortably share personal experiences. This came in handy professionally, and now that I'm retired, it helps me make friends. I enjoy taking walks on the beach and striking up conversations with others. These people start out as strangers, but soon after meeting, we freely talk, share aspects of our lives, and become friends.

4. Learn from failure. Some experiences hit you right between the eyes. These lessons might be hard to learn, but they're unforgettable. My first big shock occurred when I was a junior in college and my psychology professor arranged an interview for me to discuss a possible internship at the Port Authority of NY&NJ, one of the wealthiest public agencies in the United States. Naively, I dressed in a sweater and tie. When I arrived, I saw that everyone else was dressed in a business suit. I was horribly embarrassed and then stricken to learn that because I wasn't dressed appropriately, I wouldn't be allowed to participate in the interview.

Then and there, I vowed to learn all I could about corporate America and its values. Sure enough, as a consultant, I wore suits throughout my career. I had to fit in so that I could eventually stand out. The lesson is, when in Rome, do as the Romans do. This is wisdom I heeded throughout my career.

5. Reflect deeply. I once had a consulting failure I didn't understand for many years. I'd been asked by another consulting company to help train the senior salespeople of a highly successful drug company at a conference in Atlanta.

I knew I was in trouble from the beginning, when the managers refused to accept the hotel chef and insisted I hire a special French chef to prepare them elaborate breakfasts. It quickly became obvious that these folks had come to Atlanta to enjoy themselves and only secondarily to learn to coach their salespeople.

I finally managed to get the managers to buckle down to the planned schedule, but when the program ended, they complained about me, and the consulting company didn't hire me again to work with its client.

For years, I thought I was right to insist the program be run rigorously, even though the sales managers were content to cut corners. Years later, I realized my high standards were shortsighted. The consulting company tolerated substandard work for this program, and the drug company was making so much money that it didn't care what its salespeople were doing.

In hindsight, for the duration of the training event, I should have simply done the best I could without offending anyone. After all, the client wasn't mine. After the program, I could have dropped this assignment and given my reasons.

This unfortunate experience taught me to be very selective when choosing my own clients. Eventually, my consulting firm became known for designing high-quality programs. Sticking to my standards paid off with my own clients.

To gauge where you are on the journey toward maturity, assess how well you're doing at mastering the following qualities. Remember, you can never quite get there, and there's always room for improvement, but if you can get a handle on these qualities, you are probably as mature as you're going to get.

Six Qualities Mature People Have in Common[10]

Note: I first read about these six qualities as a young psychology student, and I encouraged my corporate clients to develop themselves accordingly

---

10. M. R. Feinberg, "Marks of Maturity," *Psychology of Administration*, 1963, 163–167.

throughout my 30-year practice. These are universal marks of personal success, in my opinion.

1. They accept themselves. If you can accept yourself with all your faults, you will enjoy yourself more because you'll like yourself. Until you can fully accept yourself, you'll likely find it hard to accept others who have faults you don't admire. Acceptance is unconditional and requires a great deal of tolerance and patience. We all get angry at others, but mature people don't attack those they find disagreeable. They also aren't overly proud, nor do they belittle themselves or others. People who are self-accepting can genuinely laugh at themselves. This makes them feel uniquely human and alive!

2. They accept others in spite of their limitations. This doesn't mean ignoring their deficiencies. In fact, accepting others helps you recognize and adapt to their faults and be even more tolerant. Mature people have no sense of guilt when they disagree with others, nor do they give in to whims in order to be liked. Mature people know they get to decide whom to be friends with. Just be careful not to get caught up in status seeking. Don't shame others if they can't do certain things as well as you can. Don't choose friends based on what they can do for you or kid yourself into believing you like someone when you don't. Pretense is a lie that will eventually cause you not to like yourself!

3. They accept help from others. Everyone wants to be independent, but we all occasionally depend on other people. It's healthy to admit we need other people. For example, asking for directions when you're lost makes sense. Going to the doctor when you're sick makes even greater sense. People who adamantly refuse to ask for help are silly. That said, it's not okay to lean on people when you don't need assistance. Taking the easy way out isn't a sign of maturity. Struggling is part of the learning process, so don't give up too quickly. Mastering life's challenges is a great way to learn independence. Just don't let your pride get the best of you.

4. They enjoy the present. Some people think a lot about the past and revel in their memories. Others spend a great deal of time worrying about the future. Still others tell themselves they'll do things differently tomorrow or even in years to come, just not now. Psychologists call enjoying the present "living in the here and now." Some days won't go right, but the sun always comes up tomorrow. That's the beauty of life. Every day is a new day on life's journey. Just don't get stuck in a rut, doing nothing new day after day. Be inquisitive, use your ingenuity, and invent new ways of living. It's up to you to take full advantage of life.

5. They practice patience and restraint. We're all born lacking impulse control. It's just how we're made. Eventually, small children learn not to touch hot stoves or put dangerous things in their mouths. Oddly enough, some adults act more like children than adults. They do unsafe things and laugh about them. College students die every day doing reckless things. Patience is almost the opposite of recklessness or impulsiveness. To master patience, you have to stop yourself from reacting, consider what you want to do, and then deliberately do it. Reacting is not the same as acting. Throughout life, step back and ask yourself, *"Am I acting or reacting?"* when you face frustrating experiences.

6. They enjoy their work. Careers today take unique twists. Most include three or more jobs. Even entrepreneurs take on new and different kinds of work as their careers progress. Most mature people find satisfaction in their careers, but psychologists know that even mundane jobs can be satisfying. It all depends on whether or not you're using your talents and feel productive and engaged. You can make work more interesting by setting goals, testing yourself, being resourceful, and inventing new ways of doing your job. This is satisfying and fun, but if the time comes that work is consistently dull and your career is going nowhere, do something about it. I'm not necessarily suggesting you quit (that would be reacting and not acting), but if you're confined to work you no longer enjoy, remember that your life is not your job. Maybe it's time to look at other jobs or seek training for a new career. Perhaps you can find rewarding things to do outside of work. Mentoring a disadvantaged child or helping those less fortunate are just two ways of giving back. For some people, these pursuits are more rewarding than their jobs.

Remember, maturity is a journey in pursuit of making life as fulfilling as possible. Are you mature? Are you on your way to maturity? In sum, here are my wisdoms for leading a mature life:

- Maturity is the one goal no human being ever quite reaches. The pursuit of maturity is what's most important, and we can each deliberately embrace opportunities to develop and become more mature.

- Immature people stumble on life experiences and just try to get by. Mature individuals know their strengths and look for opportunities to use them optimally to succeed.

- Everyone has natural skills that come easily, but most pursuits take hard work. If you have natural talent in music, for example, you likely could develop mastery faster than most people, but some aspects of playing music will still challenge you. The great composer Mozart was a child prodigy whose natural musical talent was apparent when he was young. Nonetheless, it took hard work to get his compositions just right.

- Mature people accept themselves with all their frailties. They ask for help when they need it. They do not feel inadequate for doing so, but they know that asking for too much help is no better than asking for too little help.

- Leaning on other people when you can capably do things yourself is self-defeating and limits your maturity.

- Stay in the present and invest in life. Do not spin your wheels reminiscing about the past or dwelling on the future.

- Practice patience with yourself and others. Patience requires restraint and deliberate action rather than reacting.

- Enjoy your work and the lifetime pursuit of a career. There are many ways to reinvent work if it gets boring or stale. "Boring" is a state of mind. It's up to you to make life and work interesting and rewarding.

Recommended Readings

Internet References

Banu, Sharmin. "Know Your Strengths, Capitalize on Them." *Greenleaf Leadership Coaching*, July 15, 2013. http://blog.greenleafcoach.com/2013/07/15/know-your-strenghts-capitalize-on-them/.

Bhandarkar, Sumitha. "20 Questions to Know Yourself Better and Unlock the Immense Potential Within." *Dumb Little Man*, July 12, 2013. https://www.dumblittleman.com/20-questions-to-know-yourself-better/.

Collingwood, Jane. "Capitalize on Your Core Strengths." *Psych Central*, July 17, 2016. https://psychcentral.com/lib/capitalize-on-your-core-strengths/.

Ferguson, Nicholas. "3 Reasons Why Receiving Feedback Will Help Your Personal Growth." *Nicholas Ferguson*. http://nicholasferguson.org/3-reasons-why-receiving-feedback-will-help-your-personal-growth/.

Henry, Alan. "How Can I Learn to Take Criticism without Taking It Personally?" *Lifehacker*, June 4, 2012. https://lifehacker.com/5915488/how-can-i-learn-to-take-criticism-without-taking-it-personally.

Print References

Feinberg, M. R. "Marks of Maturity." *Psychology of Administration*. 1963, 163–167.

Chapter 6:

Motivation

EVERYTHING WE DO, EVERY ACTION we take, and every goal we attempt to reach is the result of our motivations or needs. Simply put, motivation is what drives us.

When you tell someone you're in a funk and don't feel motivated to do anything, this isn't actually true; it's just how you happen to be expressing your feelings. Maybe you don't feel good or lack the energy or "get up and go," but even if you don't realize what's causing your funk, it's motivated by a need of some kind. Perhaps you need rest. Perhaps you need time alone. Perhaps you need quiet time to heal or even daydream.

Different needs can motivate you at the same time. When they combine, they often heighten your behavior to higher levels. Say a world-class tennis player is nearing the end of a hard-fought match. She wants not only to win but also to break a world record. Dual needs push her to reach her maximum.

This athlete's need to achieve is a primary driver, but perhaps she also wants to win the recognition of the world tennis association for outstanding work. The acceptance and adulation of her fans might further energize her. Finally, she might feel threatened by the possibility of losing the last big game. Anxiety can be a strong motivator that yields even greater strength.

When you think about what motivates you, think of your many different needs, not just one. These will help you become acutely aware of what drives you. Remember, understanding yourself is the basis of all wisdom.

Here's another example. Perhaps you intend to go to college and pledge a fraternity. Several needs might drive your decision. Perhaps you want to enjoy the friendship of your frat brothers, attend their social gatherings and parties, and have fun and relax at the frat house. To achieve this, first you must "pledge" and go through some grueling hurdles to win an invitation to join. Some of these hurdles are silly, and your willingness to tackle them reflects your desire to join.

Let's say you "pass" some early tests only to learn the very last challenge requires you to drink vodka straight out of a long rubber pipe. To impress everyone, you must drink as much as you can. You manage to pass the test, but another pledge gets so sick he has to be rushed to the hospital, where he nearly dies. The fellow who drank himself nearly to death was a victim of his own extreme motivation. He took a risk that could have cost him his life. You also took a risk that could have cost you your life, but you were luckier than he was.

The fact is, the closer you get to a goal, the more motivated you are to reach it. Marathon runners typically divide their races into shorter markers. Every time they get close to a marker, they naturally speed up. This psychological advantage in racing is called the goal gradient effect[11].

Say you wake up one day and wish you didn't have to go to school. As the hours pass, you find yourself less attentive and more restless and fidgety. It's not that you're tired. It's that you're coming to the end of the school day. Consequently, your impatience quickly mounts to be the first student out the door.

Human motivation is indeed complex, and psychologists have focused on the opposing emotions we all experience as our drives play out. Psychologist Richard Solomon developed a theory of motivation that explains how pairs

---

11. "Goal Gradient Effect," *Conversion Uplift*, 2017, https://www.conversion-uplift.co.uk/glossary-of-conversion-marketing/goal-gradient-effect/.

of opposing emotions work with one another[12]. Examples of his opponent-process theory include fear and relief, pleasure and pain, and feelings of security or threat.

Solomon observed that when one emotion is experienced, the opposite emotion is suppressed. For example, he analyzed the emotions present when beginning skydivers jumped from a plane. Initially their fears were extreme, but as they repeated their jumps, their fears decreased and their pleasure increased.

In another example, say you are approached by an aggressive dog. The emotion of fear quickly takes over and relief is non-existent. If the dog stays nearby but doesn't attack, your fear eventually decreases and your feelings of relief intensify. If the dog disappears, your fear disappears altogether and you are flooded with relief.

Feelings likewise often run in opposing pairs when we experience great motivation, and teens in particular typically have a difficult time understanding what it all means or how to control it. This might explain a number of thrill-seeking behaviors many teens engage in, including risky behaviors that cause fatal accidents and even drug addictions.

For example, psychologists have found that taking addictive drugs such as cocaine and heroin can produce extreme pleasurable feelings, but after taking them, negative emotions occur. Eventually, drug users take their drugs not so much for the pleasure they experience in the moment but to avoid the terrible withdrawal symptoms they experience when the moment ends.

I hope no millennial reading this book will ever experiment with addictive drugs, but if you do, understand that conflicting emotions might control your behavior and increase and/or dampen your motivation in a cyclical way as time goes by.

---

12. "Opponent-Process Theory," *Exploring Psychology*, http://mhhe.com/cls/psy/ch10/opponent.mhtml.

Many drivers will recall similar feelings of intense desire and pleasure when they first began looking forward to driving a car. Waiting for that day to arrive was tough! Recall how your motivation heightened as it drew near and at long last arrived? At first, you loved the thrill of driving, but eventually the experience became routine. Perhaps one day you got into your car and found that you were bored, restless, or maybe irresistibly curious about how fast it could go. In other words, you wanted to experience the "thrill" of driving fast to relieve your boredom.

Note how the emotion accompanying "the thrill" is the opposite of the emotion of boredom. Risky behavior is at work, and this time, it impacts the safety of others around you as well as your own safety. As mentioned earlier, teen brains are not fully developed, and sometimes it seems the brains of adults aren't, either. Please don't let momentary "thrills" compromise your good judgment. Our emotions often reflect great joy, but do your best to avoid risky behavior, which can be dangerous in more ways than one.

Clearly, motivation is a two-edged sword. It works best when you're energized to reach a goal, but you must exercise good judgment and restraint as you get close to reaching this point. Unfortunately, since adolescent brains are still maturing, good judgment and restraint can be elusive. Here's my advice for adolescents: make no goal so compelling that it consumes you, distracts you, or compromises your good judgment.

Motivated behavior is especially critical early in life. When a baby first nurses or drinks from a bottle, the sucking response appears to be quite natural and automatic. As the baby learns from trial and error, the sucking response becomes more efficient. Learning happens fast!

The famous psychologist B. F. Skinner conducted landmark experiments with lab rats in which he withheld food pellets until the rats were so hungry they began searching for pellets everywhere in their cages[13]. When they accidentally touched a lever near the food and a pellet dropped, the rats

---

13. Saul MacLeod, "Skinner–Operant Conditioning," *Simply Psychology*, 2015, https://www.simplypsychology.org/operant-conditioning.html.

voraciously ate it. Eventually, the rats learned to press the lever to get the pellets, and soon they'd learned all kinds of tricks. We all learn from satisfying one need or another. Learning is motivated behavior.

Like the rats, when you get very hungry, you search quickly through your refrigerator and gobble what you find until you're sated. At this point, your hunger motivation drops to near zero, but what if there were no food anywhere you looked? What if a natural disaster cut off your food supply? What if you were lost and stranded in a remote forest with nothing to eat?

You would eat almost anything, and the power of your motivation to find food would consume you. The smartest people stranded in the remote forest would survive using their wits and resourcefulness, including their knowledge of survival skills. Other smart learners would quickly learn from them. Human motivation makes us ever more adept and shrewd.

I've known doctors and medical researchers who seek cures for rare diseases. My wife died from the rare disease myotonic dystrophy. I've seen firsthand how hard and long medical people toil for breakthroughs, working year after year to crack the code of specific diseases. These people are driven!

Psychologists find that the goals of these highly dedicated people are specific, measurable, attainable, and highly rewarding, even though they invariably experience both successes and failures.

Measurable goals are very powerful. For example, when I began exercising with my trainer, she had me do routines until I was tired. Eventually, I found myself losing interest and just going through the motions. I decided to change things up by asking her to grade each routine from "A" to "F."

As she graded me, I began to work harder, and I also became interested in tracking myself. In other words, I became an active learner. After a while, I mastered certain exercises and asked my trainer to teach me new ones. I didn't want "A"s all the time unless I was making progress!

Accomplishing easy tasks isn't motivating, nor is attempting near-impossible tasks. You need to press yourself to new but achievable limits to maximize your learning in life. You should also celebrate small wins, as this is crucial in keeping momentum going. It also helps build enthusiastic teams. Sometimes when you least expect it, you will succeed beyond your wildest dreams, and other times when you fully expect to succeed, you won't.

A classic business study found that workers who didn't expect promotions but got them anyway were more satisfied than workers who fully expected promotions and did in fact get them[14]. If you think you will succeed all the time, you're in for some big disappointments. It's better to set demanding goals and press yourself to accomplish them and just hope you'll be rewarded fairly.

The good news is, regardless of the career you choose, you are highly likely to experience setbacks and advances. Why do I call this good news? Because it's more motivating to have ups and downs than most people realize. Think of famous movie stars. The fact that they make great movies along with the occasional flop motivates them.

Indeed, research confirms that life's highs and lows are more motivating than a steady diet of successes. In addition, variable reinforcement in the form of unexpected rewards is even more motivating than other types of rewards. If you're fortunate and talented, you might have more highs than lows, but the occasional flop will spur you on while giving you ample opportunity to use your resourcefulness.

It's worth noting that from a motivation standpoint, it's far more effective to make skills-based evaluations than personality-based ones. This is true whether you're evaluating others or evaluating yourself. For example, say "She's working to spruce up her public speaking skills" rather than "She's a lousy public speaker." About yourself, say "I'm currently working on my math skills" rather than "I suck at math." This keeps the door open for all kinds of breakthroughs instead of slamming the door in someone's—possibly your own—face.

---

14. Kurt Lewin, "Psychology of Success and Failure," in *Psychology in Administration*, ed. T. W. Costello and S. H. Zalkind (Englewood Cliffs, NJ: Prentice-Hall, Inc., 1963), 67–78.

The fact is, achievements don't just happen. They depend on your talents, the opportunities you pursue, and your motivation. Individuals vary widely in achievement motivation. High achievers generally have higher self-esteem than the average person. Psychologists have studied individuals with high achievement drives[15]. It's easy to spot these individuals just by watching what they do:

- They step up and assume responsibility for making decisions, which they consider to be an opportunity for achievement.
- They take moderate risks when the outcome depends on skill, not on chance.
- They operate best after receiving specific feedback on whether or not they've been successful.
- They tend to "think ahead" about possible challenges, and they enjoy anticipating how they will manage them.
- They are not overly confident. They worry about failure, but that doesn't stop them. In fact, it increases their motivation even more.

Whether you realize it or not, the groups you join and the friends you spend time with can drag you down or increase your achievement motivation. When I was in grammar school, my friends were mediocre students and my grades weren't very good. When I started middle school, I discovered I loved algebra, and I got the best grade in class. This was the first time I realized I wanted to be excellent at something! Eventually, I made high school friends who wanted to go to college. Some of these classmates were really bright, and later on, my college buddies were, too. I wanted to get grades as good as or better than theirs. Now I had a clear, measurable goal, and I enjoyed testing the limits of my academic performance against my friends'. My grades got

---

15. "McClelland Achievement and Acquired Needs Theory," *Your Coach*, 2018, https://www.yourcoach.be/en/employee-motivation-theories/mcclelland-achievement-and-acquired-needs-motivation-theory.php.

better and better, and they helped me get into Columbia University for my graduate work. Achievement motivation paid off, and my self-confidence did, too. In fact, my graduate studies weren't nearly as difficult as other students found them to be.

In sum, here are my motivation wisdoms:

- Everything you do in life or think about doing is motivated by a need. You might or might not be aware of what needs are driving your actions.

- Most behavior is driven by several motivations rather than one. If you ask yourself probing questions, you might discover what needs you are attempting to satisfy. This requires self-examination. Some motivations will be obvious, but others won't be. Sometimes the light will dawn on you when you least expect it to.

- When a number of strong needs drives your behavior, you will be even more motivated, both emotionally and physically, to succeed.

- When goals are measurable and clear, you become energized as you get closer to reaching them because your motivation heightens. Be very careful to exercise restraint as you near the goal. Some people go into overdrive, which causes them to act impulsively or even dangerously right before reaching it.

- When goals are too easy or appear impossible, they aren't motivating. Everyone experiences success and failure. A bumpy journey toward a goal generally increases your motivation and can be a test of your resourcefulness.

- Individuals with a high achievement drive do things differently than other people and aren't easily discouraged. They are always looking for future opportunities to accomplish still greater challenges. While they have the same fears of failure that everyone else has, their anxieties drive them to push themselves harder to accomplish goals that are extremely difficult for most of us.

Recommended Readings

Internet References

"Goal Gradient Effect." *Conversion Uplift*, 2017. https://www.conversion-uplift.co.uk/glossary-of-conversion-marketing/goal-gradient-effect/.

MacLeod, Saul. "Skinner–Operant Conditioning." *Simply Psychology*, 2015. https://www.simplypsychology.org/operant-conditioning.html.

"McClelland Achievement and Acquired Needs Theory." *Your Coach*, 2018. https://www.yourcoach.be/en/employee-motivation-theories/mcclelland-achievement-and-acquired-needs-motivation-theory.php.

"McClelland's Theory of Needs." *Net MBA*, 2010. http://www.netmba.com/mgmt/ob/motivation/mcclelland/.

"Motivation." *Psychology Today*. https://www.psychologytoday.com/us/basics/motivation.

"Need for Achievement." *Wikipedia*, last modified January 20, 2018. https://en.wikipedia.org/wiki/Need_for_achievement, accessed April 9, 2018.

"Opponent-Process Theory." *Exploring Psychology*. http://mhhe.com/cls/psy/ch10/opponent.mhtml.

Print References

Lewin, Kurt. "Psychology of Success and Failure." *Psychology in Administration*, edited by T. W. Costello and S. H. Zalkind, 67–78. Englewood Cliffs, NJ: Prentice-Hall, Inc., 1963.

SECTION III:

Life Skills to Cultivate throughout Adulthood

Chapter 7:

Leadership

THERE IS NO DOUBT THE WORLD has benefitted from great leaders. Gandhi was a great change leader. He won India's independence from Great Britain and the hearts of millions of his fellow countrymen. They rallied behind him even as Britain imposed all kinds of sanctions, including imprisonment, to suppress his efforts.

You likely know a number of great leaders from history. Often they came from very modest beginnings, such as Abraham Lincoln and Martin Luther King Jr. These people had tremendous vision and courage. They faced incredible opposition, but they prevailed and changed the core beliefs of many, leaving lasting legacies for all to benefit from. Like Gandhi, these individuals were successful "change leaders."

History has also had its share of great "crisis leaders" who emerged when we needed them the most. President Franklin D. Roosevelt came to office during the Great Depression when more than a quarter of Americans had been out of work for three years. Having lost nearly everything they had, people were overcome with fear and a sense of demonization. The country needed a leader who possessed strong conviction and optimism and could get people to believe in him. Sure enough, FDR moved boldly to pull the country out of the Depression. Although he faced doubters and fierce political opposition, he was a source of inspiration when there was no hope. In one famous radio speech, he said, "We have nothing to fear but fear itself." While this was far from true, it gave the masses something to believe in when many thought the Depression would never end.

Both change leaders and crisis leaders share many qualities. Typically, their leadership is challenged every step of the way, they exhibit unwavering conviction and purpose, they can visualize exactly where they are leading people, and their messages grip people emotionally. In different ways, these leaders influence how others think.

You might never face the overwhelming odds these great historical leaders faced, but you will have ample opportunity to lead other people throughout your lifetime. You actually learn some principles of leadership in school, though you might not realize it. In addition to teaching specific subjects, your teachers lead your classes. Some of them motivate you to want to do your best just so you won't disappoint them. Nearly all of them expect you to follow where they lead.

Keep in mind that "following" isn't always bad. It's a great way to learn about leadership, and successful followers can be valuable partners to leaders. For example, sharing constructive feedback is something followers often do (so do leaders), and followers often take opportunities to become leaders down the road. Both roles are critical to the success of teams.

All leaders exercise leadership differently, and different situations call for different types of leadership. A basketball coach leads a team. A school principal leads teachers and staff. A business executive leads employees who might be spread all over the globe. It's not possible to successfully lead all these people the same way, yet in each case, leadership is an ongoing process of influencing others based on a vision that emanates from the leader and connects with his or her followers.

A leader's task is thus threefold: envision, energize, execute. Without a vision, leaders are actually glorified managers. If leaders are successful, their expectations are accepted and embraced, but few leaders manage this easily, as attempts at resistance and even confrontation are common. At times, the resistance is subtle. The most difficult resistance occurs when people say nothing directly but meet on their own to plan how to stop or even undermine the leader.

For some, leadership comes naturally, but leadership can be learned. Managers read about it, attend training courses, and seek coaching to sharpen their skills. If you want to assume a leadership role, here are some suggestions for how you might proceed:

- You can practice leadership skills on a small scale, such as by organizing a day trip.

- You can accept assignments that make you the point person on a project.

- You can become a member of a team but assume a leadership role if your group is floundering and needs clearer direction.

- You can offer special expertise that others might need.

Keep in mind that having expertise doesn't mean your leadership will be accepted or even wanted. If you are promoted to a leadership position that requires you to lead other people, be careful! Even if you're a recognized expert, there's no guarantee you'll be able to effectively lead. On the other hand, without expertise, your leadership simply won't be accepted. Imagine a big league baseball manager trying to lead his team with very little knowledge of the game. However, big league managers don't have to be big league stars. Other leadership skills can be even more important. In fact, every big league team relies on several expert coaches the managers call on for advice.

There are many ways to lead others. Some will be comfortable for you and some won't, but certain skills make for outstanding leaders. You've probably already learned a few of these in school, sports, or jobs, but you can always try to get better at them.

Barry M. Cohen, PhD

Skills Outstanding Leaders Have in Common

1. They communicate with others. This doesn't merely mean they talk with or persuade others. After all, many good salespeople aren't good leaders. Effective communicators tune into people, recognize what they care most about, talk to them easily, encourage them to freely exchange ideas, and in short come across as approachable.

2. They listen to others. The best leaders listen to what is said and also to what is not said. They listen to underlying feelings that aren't explicitly conveyed. They sense when individuals are confused or conflicted and gently bring their concerns to the table. The best leaders are patient, mature, and restrained. Typically, others admire them for these leadership qualities.

3. They motivate others to achieve success. They do this by discovering other people's talents and recognizing and rewarding their contributions. Everyone has unique needs that energize them. If you can identify these needs, you can frame your leadership attempts accordingly. Some people love solving problems and using their ingenuity while others are better at helping people organize and monitoring the team's efforts toward a goal. As you get to know the individuals on your team, you will learn what their unique talents and needs are. The best leaders have a knack for getting the team's combined resources to work in sync toward shared goals.

4. They lead with flexibility and independence. This is a challenge for most leaders. On the one hand, they must set the ship on course and provide direction. On the other hand, they must be open to mid-course corrections. They must also deal with those who resist them. This takes assertiveness mixed with flexibility. If leaders become obsessed with their own ideas, their credibility suffers, sometimes beyond the point of recovery. Yet leaders have to stand out from their teams. If they don't maintain their independence, they can lose just as much credibility. The trick is learning the art of applying independence and flexibility at just the right times. Those who become top managers have the added responsibility of leading many people. At this point, they rely greatly on their executive leadership team. This job tests their resourcefulness and maturity and requires a number of talents that some leaders struggle to learn for years. Note: I have not counseled a single executive who is great at all of them!

5. They make executive impact. This is the ability to make a positive impression on people quickly, on contact. It is also the ability to make a lasting impact on large groups such as employees, stockholders, and major customers through speeches, conversations, and media exposure. The best leaders have the uncanny ability to get people to like them and trust them even when they have little personal contact. President Ronald Reagan made this type of impact. An actor before he was elected president, he had an informal style of communication that people all over the country liked. He made even complex subjects understandable and took stances that were crystal clear. For example, think of his famous speech at the Berlin Wall when he turned to the Russian premier and said, "Mr. Gorbachev, tear down this wall!" This symbolic shot of freedom was heard around the world. Two years later, the wall was taken down and Berlin was reunited.

6. They display executive judgment. The problems that reach the executive team are complex and fraught with uncertainties and risks. Consequently, the senior team consists of intelligent people with experience in different disciplines. The top executive might meet with consultants or leading executives of other companies to gain outside perspectives. Remember, smart people ask for help when they need it. This isn't a sign of weakness. It takes maturity and a willingness to check assumptions. After all, everyone has blind spots.

7. They develop talent. The senior team is responsible for developing people. These individuals are often called on to mentor or coach promising mid-level managers. Developing top talent ensures that the organization will have a strong bench and "ready now" replacements. Organizations with cultures that encourage professional growth and development attract talented people! Years ago, IBM earned the reputation of moving people frequently to develop them, so much so that for a time, it became known as the "I have been moved" (short for IBM) company.

8. They think strategically. Because the senior team is responsible for charting the future course of the organization, outstanding leaders are superb future thinkers. Remember, life is full of chances and there are no guarantees. Anyone can guess at the future, but talented strategic thinkers make new possibilities happen. They can call on other experts to quantify what is known in the marketplace, but deciding a future direction means stepping into new and untried territory where initiatives are brand new. Being a strong planner helps, but strategic thinking is far more complex.

You might wonder whether you would enjoy managing other people. The great psychologist David McClelland devoted his entire career to studying the motivations of workers[16]. He identified three needs that drive all of us, needs that have been validated by a great deal of research. You can gauge how these needs drive you now, but do it again once you start looking for a career that interests you and yet again when you're in the middle of your career and wondering if it's truly a good fit.

Three Needs That Drive Human Beings

1. Need for achievement. Remember this one? I confess, I have this need in abundance. People with a need for achievement thrive on demanding challenges and seek solutions to difficult problems. They enjoy setting and accomplishing attainable goals and tracking their progress. They are moderate risk takers. In teams, they assume responsibility for the work of the team and organize others to make the team more productive. They are often entrepreneurs and managers, and sometimes they get so addicted to their work that they become workaholics. Everyone needs a healthy balance

---

16. "McClelland Achievement and Acquired Needs Theory," *Your Coach*, 2018, https://www.yourcoach.be/en/employee-motivation-theories/mcclelland-achievement-and-acquired-needs-motivation-theory.php.

of work and leisure, but finding that balance is a challenge for many high achievers.

2. Need for power. These people thrive on influencing others. They enjoy status and work hard to reach the rank they want to attain. Not surprisingly, executives typically have high power needs that often exceed their achievement needs as they seek to influence and energize others to follow them. Mature executives do not abuse power; they apply self-restraint. Immature executives are extremely competitive and will do everything possible to advance, even at the expense of others or the best interests of the organization. Power-hungry executives are similar to workaholics because they have insatiable drives that simply can't be fully met.

3. Need for affiliation. These individuals thrive on teamwork and collaboration. They have a deep desire to belong. They are not comfortable judging, confronting, or disciplining others. They can lead other people, but they prefer to have those they know and trust do the leading. Executives often rely on these individuals for counsel and trust them for their loyalty.

Looking back, it's clear that my career as a consulting psychologist fit me very well. I am not particularly competitive, nor do I have the slightest interest in status or self-promotion. I am extremely loyal, and I have a natural ability to get all kinds of people to trust me. I enjoy accomplishing things and work very hard to achieve excellence, but I'm far more competitive with and demanding of myself than I am with others. In short, I have high achievement needs and moderately high affiliation needs but a moderately low need for power.

The following case study offers a closer look at leadership in the form of one unique man who took the helm of one of the most challenging turnarounds in aviation history.

Barry M. Cohen, PhD

Leadership in Action: A Case Study[17]

I first met Ed Northern shortly after he was recruited from General Electric Company to lead the transformation of aerospace manufacturer Pratt & Whitney's jet engine business. Ed was no stranger to turbine engines or the aviation industry. He brought an envious GE track record in lean manufacturing, but his expertise could not account for his extraordinary leadership in turning around Pratt's flailing manufacturing organization.

Pratt & Whitney's engine business had dominated the market for several years. The company had installed more than 15,000 commercial jet engines, serving almost 500 customers around the globe. In fact, the jet engine business alone posted sales of 5.8 billion dollars and was the very profitable flagship of the huge conglomerate United Technologies (UTC).

When you board a jet airplane and look out the window, you cannot miss the huge engines on the sides and rear of the plane. Pratt & Whitney's engines were very profitable because maintaining them required spare parts and service overhauls, too. Hence, the business expanded greatly beyond the sale of the initial product.

The aviation industry suffered drastic cutbacks for orders beginning in 1990. The Cold War was ending, and military orders for engines greatly decreased. At the same time, the commercial airline industry faced huge cuts marked by major airline liquidations. Notably, five carriers filed for bankruptcy.

Pratt began scrambling for business, as did the other titans in the jet engine business, General Electric and Rolls Royce. Competition became intense, and although Pratt began with a comfortable share of the market,

---

17. A. Burris, S. Rykebusch, and J. Schiavone, "Transformation of Pratt & Whitney North Haven (A)," *Harvard Business Review* (November 28, 1995): Business Case 9-696-066.

the company lacked the innovation and cost competitiveness to win new business. It soon became apparent that Pratt was losing the race.

Unable to deliver low-cost, on-time deliveries of the most fuel-efficient engines in order to dominate the marketplace, the manufacturing organization suffered unbearable stress. With employee cutbacks needed, morale fell fast. Even worse, employee trust sank to an all-time low. Then, in the midst of wild rumors that the jet engine business would be sold to General Electric Company, Pratt & Whitney embarked on a huge transformation. UTC's CEO assembled an entirely new team of very talented general managers, several from outside the company. Ed Northern was put in charge of jet engine manufacturing, the most costly part of Pratt's business.

I first met Ed at a leadership program that all the new general managers attended. He had been on the job just a few months and was already gaining a reputation as a forward-thinking executive determined to implement world-class lean manufacturing practices at Pratt & Whitney.

Ed made a memorable first impression. The black leather jacket he wore screamed "I am nothing like the buttoned-down managers or other 'suits' that work here," and his Southern drawl, casual demeanor, and approachable style all completed his initial positive impact. My coaching work with him began quickly as he explained the mandate he'd been given. He was assured but not cocky as he explained that his immediate priority was to establish trust throughout the organization.

To break down barriers, Ed planned to spend a great deal of time walking around all three shifts on the shop floor. He wanted to better understand the concerns of all his employees, from rank-and-file workers to supervisors and managers to everyone in between. He wanted to listen to everyone, and that included a wide swath of employees composed of engineers, quality-control technicians, project leaders, and many others.

As I followed Ed's turnaround efforts, he shared with me the leadership challenges he faced. Traditionally, Pratt managers ran operations autocratically, and it was common to threaten employees with termination. This precedent simply added a great deal more stress to the dire shape of the business. Moreover, it was unheard of to ask for anyone's opinions on how to improve the way business was done, but Ed exemplified the antithesis of the autocratic leader and was a consultative leader from day one. He told his cynical employees, "You're going to have a voice around here," and acted decisively after receiving their advice and ideas. In his first few weeks, he scheduled one-on-ones with both salaried and hourly employees. Based on the feedback he received, he quickly fired two senior managers. At that, people began to take him seriously. Ed was beginning to transform attitudes based on his unwillingness to tolerate people who blocked his vision.

Meanwhile, manufacturing had to aggressively cut costs with a series of layoffs and by eliminating or consolidating operations. This took a great deal of resourcefulness, and Ed demonstrated an abundance of this skill. For example, he drastically reorganized the "product centers" so that each assumed responsibility for a family of jet engine parts. Accordingly, each product center was provided with experts in all technical areas, rendering each center fully self-sustaining. For the first time, each center had clear, measurable goals. Ed knew that to motivate his employees to do their very best work, they needed both resources and challenging goals that would become yardsticks of progress and success. Furthermore, it was decided that the entire manufacturing process would be placed in four product lines based on common processes. These lines would be U-shaped in order to make all operations visible to all operators, creating a vehicle for instant communication and a mental identity for each team to further bring people together.

However, Ed's skillful leadership exemplified far more than organizational efficiencies. Ed became the captain of the ship, and people looked to him to chart the course. He began by articulating his vision, which consisted of seven critical elements that he believed represented world-class manufacturing. These were as follows:

1. Leadership
2. Organizing around product cells
3. Worker empowerment
4. Just-in-time manufacturing
5. Materials management planning

6. Total quality management
7. Standardization

To achieve these critical elements, Ed was determined to get the best out of his people. He believed in motivating employees to go beyond what they expected of themselves. He believed people were capable of extraordinary things, and his managers thrived on his leadership. In reality, he believed he worked for his people, not the other way around.

You can imagine how energized Ed's employees became. Simply put, Ed brought life to a dying organization. He often said his job entailed clearing away obstacles so that his employees could be successful. He provided them with the best resources available, asked them to step up and perform at their best, and coached them in his usual informal style, often repeating his mantra that "Teaching is learning twice." Above all, he listened. Pratt & Whitney's dictatorial milieu evaporated slowly at first but then surprisingly quickly, replaced with a highly open climate in which communication flowed freely and innovation was the norm and often celebrated.

Ed not only preached employee development as a strategy to remain competitive in the demanding aviation marketplace, but he insisted on it at all levels of the organization, and he exemplified this principle himself at every turn. For example, his one-on-ones always contained new teaching points, he brought in manufacturing experts from Japan to teach and implement the business philosophy of Kaizen, and despite enormous workloads, he insisted his managers attend the leadership development center to learn more about their own strengths and how to use them to support the new change initiatives in the organization.

A closer look at Ed Northern reveals how he exemplified the characteristics of all outstanding leaders.

- *They communicate with others.* Ed not only communicated with his people top to bottom, but he was also open to their feedback at every turn. He ran all employee meetings. He held one-on-ones regularly and often. He developed a "business council" of his general managers and encouraged them to work collaboratively with one another. The dictatorial environment and traditionalism of the organization he inherited was literally replaced as he began a sustained effort to transform Pratt manufacturing.

- *They listen to others.* Without "active listening," Ed Northern could not have possibly achieved the trust of his people. They resisted him at the beginning and some even refused to believe he would last, but his actions spoke loudly. He not only listened to people, but he valued their input, and he treated everyone's feedback with respect.

- *They motivate others to achieve success.* Ed Northern set challenging and measurable goals. He gave his people all the resources they needed to achieve his vision, and he believed they could achieve far beyond their own expectations. Resourcefulness was key, and employee development was valued at every opportunity. Everyone had strengths to offer, but people needed challenging opportunities to deliver, and that was how Ed Northern defined his own success—by his ability to remove obstacles and challenge people to perform. By teaching them when they asked to get better and giving them the skills they needed to succeed. Sure enough, many of his employees performed well beyond their own expectations.

- *They lead with flexibility and independence.* In my coaching with Ed, I found him singularly committed to his vision of implementing world-class manufacturing, but he also realized that key segments would take skillful leadership. Upgrading his workforce was essential. In other words, he needed to flexibly guide his people based on their readiness to learn lean manufacturing practices.

- *They make executive impact.* Ed knew his style quite well. He was not a "Madison Avenue executive" by any means. Rather, his casual, informal style worked very well, especially with rank-and-file employees. His engineering people and other professionals came to admire his extensive expertise in manufacturing, but he was also well read in a variety of areas, including psychology, leadership, and a full range of business subjects.

- *They display executive judgment.* Ed was a problem solver who was smart enough to realize what he knew and what he did not know. He consistently surrounded himself with intelligent people, and he had the maturity to rely on others who were more accomplished in areas that were not his strengths. For example, he relied on his trusted key engineers for highly detailed work, such as keeping tabs on any manufacturing processes that needed his careful attention.

- *They think strategically.* Ed knew he needed to move mountains, and he did so. Did he present a well-developed strategic plan? I doubt it. But his vision clearly spelled out the core segments for organizational improvements necessary for an outstanding manufacturing organization. Remember, as I said, all leaders face very different situations and must adjust accordingly. Ed did not need a highly developed business strategy to succeed. What he needed most was an abundance of wisdom to apply his leadership skills to bring about major change, and that he had in spades.

Here are some of the striking results Ed achieved at Pratt in just six months:

- Productivity increased by 47%
- Lead times decreased by 50%
- Quality increased by 89%
- Inventory reductions reached 30%

Years after Ed's retirement, he explained to me that Pratt's turbine airfoils business lines comprised 1% of all of UTC's business lines, 5% of the corporation's employment, and 35% of its income in the years the turnaround occurred. Furthermore, he noted that several of the key managers in his business council had gone on to enjoy subsequent leadership careers in such global businesses as Honeywell, Allied Signal, and General Electric. He was even more proud of their many accomplishments than of his own. Truly, Ed Northern left a legacy in American manufacturing history.

If you're interested in learning more about what extraordinary change leaders do, try watching a few great movies. *Twelve Angry Men* (1957) examines a jury charged with deciding whether a young man murdered his father. The jury chairman asks for a vote before the evidence is even discussed. Only one jurist, played by Henry Fonda, votes not to convict. He is tasked with gradually and patiently swaying the jury's thinking in this outstanding movie highlighting great leadership.

In *Poseidon Adventure* (1972), the SS *Poseidon* cruise ship is capsized in a huge tidal wave. Passengers are trapped and killed below deck while others panic and search for ways to escape. With only a few pockets of air remaining, time is running out. A minister played by the actor Gene Hackman leads a group of passengers through an incredible series of life-and-death situations in a stellar example of crisis leadership.

In *Gandhi* (1982), Ben Kingsley plays the young lawyer who left South Africa and returned to his native country only to struggle alongside his fellow countrymen against British rule. In spite of being imprisoned for testing the authority of officials and the police, the resolute Gandhi creates a form of opposition called non-violent resistance and the masses follow him until India is finally granted her independence. Gandhi's remarkable example of resourcefulness and non-violent resistance was subsequently practiced by many other great change leaders, including Martin Luther King Jr.

In sum, here are my wisdoms on leadership:

- Change leaders and crisis leaders have great resolve against people or forces that threaten their efforts. These leaders rise to the occasion when their leadership is needed most and can seemingly appear out of nowhere.

- All leaders exercise leadership differently. Much depends on the situations they face and the jobs they do. Individuals must find the leadership roles that fit their unique personalities and talents.

- Successful leaders need a certain amount of expertise if others are to find them credible. However, expertise is no guarantee of leadership success, nor is persuasiveness a guarantee of success. Leadership takes far greater skills.

- Managers who are responsible for directing other people are expected to be leaders, but the skills needed to lead successfully have to be learned from experience, training, and coaching. Some managers don't make good leaders, while others discover their best talents when leading. Self-discovery is a great way to build the wisdom muscles it takes to be a leader!

- The skills needed to be a manager must be mastered before that manager is ready for an executive job. Individuals promoted prematurely or for the wrong reasons fail; this hurts everyone. Executive skills are complex and challenging. Most executives spend their entire careers developing these talents. The best executives are open to learning and have the wisdom to know what they don't know. They seek counsel from trusted people inside and outside the organization.

- Turnaround leaders exemplify all the skills of accomplished managers. Additionally, they have an uncanny ability to orchestrate their skills to empower others to push the envelope to greater heights that surprise even them. These very talented leaders leave a legacy in their organizations for all to admire.

- You will likely work most of your life. If you find yourself in a career that isn't satisfying, it might be time to look elsewhere. Understanding yourself is the source of wisdom. Start by examining your motivations for achievement, power, and affiliation. Everyone has a unique combination of these three needs.

Barry M. Cohen, PhD

Recommended Readings

Internet References

"Contingency Theory." *Wikipedia,* last modified March 18, 2018. https://en.wikipedia.org/w/index.php?title=Contingency_theory&oldid=831102654, accessed April 9, 2018.

Hanson, Baron Christopher. "Why Followership Is the New Leadership." *Switch and Shift*, July 28, 2014. http://switchandshift.com/why-followership-is-the-new-leadership.

"McClelland Achievement and Acquired Needs Theory." *Your Coach*, 2018. https://www.yourcoach.be/en/employee-motivation-theories/mcclelland-achievement-and-acquired-needs-motivation-theory.php.

Prior, Robert. "5 Leadership Skills We Can Learn from 5 Great NFL Coaches." *Northeastern University*, 2017. https://cps.northeastern.edu/blog/story/5-leadership-skills-we-can-learn-5-great-nfl-coaches.

Riggio, Ronald E. "The Top 10 Leadership Competencies." *Psychology Today*, April 27, 2014. https://www.psychologytoday.com/us/blog/cutting-edge-leadership/201404/the-top-10-leadership-competencies.

"The Five Practices of Exemplary Leadership Model." *The Leadership Challenge*, 2018. http://www.leadershipchallenge.com/about-section-our-approach.aspx.

"World's Most Admired Companies." *Fortune*. http://archive.fortune.com/magazines/fortune/most-admired/2012/full_list/.

Print References

Bennis, Warren. *Strategies for Taking Charge*. Harper & Row. 1985.

Burris, A., S. Rykebusch, and J. Schiavone. "Transformation of Pratt & Whitney North Haven (A)." *Harvard Business Review*. November 28, 1995, Business Case 9-696-066.

Chapter 8:

Active Listening

IF YOUR HEARING IS WORKING PROPERLY, you can listen, but this doesn't make you an active listener. An active listener is someone who listens for complete understanding of the message being sent.

When listening is done well, others know they have been heard. They consequently become more receptive to sharing their thoughts and feelings and are more likely to trust and respect you.

Exactly what does an active listener do? To answer the question, you need to understand the many nuances of listening. All messages have two parts, the substance of the message and the tone of the message. When you listen for substance, you process the message to determine exactly what is being said. When you process the message for tone, you determine how it is being sent. With conviction? Trust? Respect? Or possibly with skepticism? Impatience? Frustration?

You get the picture. The tones can vary almost infinitely, and they can change in a heartbeat, depending on how you respond to the people who send the message to you.

Here's a quick way to tune into human tones. Turn off the volume on your TV and watch one of the leadership movies I mentioned in the previous chapter. Pay attention to how tones are sent non-verbally. Try to recognize the feelings of the people communicating with one another. At first, this might seem strange, but you will soon recognize many attitudes.

Of course, even more information is conveyed if you listen to the tone of what you hear. In fact, body language and vocal sounds make up about 80% of all human communication! If someone is teaching you, demonstrating something, or giving a report, the substance of what is being conveyed is important, but it's hard to listen to substance alone. People tire easily, lose concentration, and even get drowsy just listening for content. Listening for tone keeps us listening for more, which is why accomplished active listeners focus on substance and tone simultaneously. Great leaders perfect this to an art form.

The best listeners frequently use what is called non-judgmental listening. They listen without judging the message or the person sending it. They also stay clear of criticizing or even giving their own opinions unless asked. By disciplining themselves this way, the person doing the talking is encouraged to explore openly and to share more.

Conversely, people hit with very direct judgmental opinions tend to quickly become defensive and even close down. If you want to learn a lot, steer clear of judgmental listening!

Non-judgmental listening is a tool used widely by professionals and consultants. Here are a few non-evaluative approaches I used to connect with my clients, especially if they were strongly opinionated or seemed resistant about a topic we were discussing:

- Invite more input with sentences such as, "Tell me more about [reference whatever it is you heard the person saying]… "

- Invite greater critical thinking with sentences such as, "What makes you say that?" (You can be more specific by referencing what you heard.)

- Ask the messenger for advice or help with sentences such as, "I am confused about… " or "Help me clarify why you believe that." (Again, reference what you heard.)

- Ask about the tone you hear with sentences such as, "I sense you are upset [or hurt/angry/pleased]. Can you please tell me why you feel this way?"

You don't want to overuse these approaches, but using them judiciously yields benefits. You will likely be seen as more credible and understanding because people tend to be more receptive to non-evaluative listeners and more open to their ideas and suggestions.

Once you're skilled at using non-judgmental listening, you're ready to learn some counseling skills that will help you help others discover their own solutions to problems.

First, make certain the person truly wants to figure out what can be done to lessen the problem at hand. In other words, be sure the individual wants to use you as a sounding board.

Be especially careful not to give your recommendations before they're asked for and before you feel qualified to render an informed opinion. Even then, be sure to offer your advice slowly and to listen actively for the other person's acceptance of your ideas. People who accept others' solutions too quickly or reject them entirely often want others to take responsibility for their solutions. In other words, they just want to pass the problem on to you!

Once you're certain someone wants your help, you can try using the following counseling skills. Happily, they work for individuals at all stages of life, from children to teens to college graduates and beyond.

How to Counsel Those Who Truly Want Your Help

1. **Ask open-ended questions that invite discussion, not yes-or-no questions that can be answered with a single word.** Also stay away from closed questions that suggest the answers *you* want to hear. For example, avoid things like, "Don't you think your problem is exaggerated by your own imagination?"

2. **Use silence wisely.** If you can get comfortable with silence, you will be surprised at how someone struggling with a problem will begin to sort things out on his or her own. Just give people time to express their feelings, and above all do not interrupt them, even with a "Yes" or a "No."

3. **Ask clarifying questions to probe the problem and then ask follow-up questions to get closer to the core.** The best detectives ask clarifying questions from different angles without implying which

track they're after.

4. **Probe for understanding of what lies at the core of the problem.** For example, you might say, "I believe what is bothering you the most is [fill in the blank]. Is that how you feel?" or "You always seem to come back to your difficulty with [fill in the blank]. If you could figure out how to deal with this person, would you feel more confident handling the problem yourself?"

The discussion that ensues can yield helpful insights and ideas that aid problem solving.

Active listening is indeed a powerful tool, and leaders especially need this skill since it's key to understanding those they lead. Then again, couples need this skill just as much as leaders do.

I knew a couple that truly was in love with one another. The woman very much valued her therapist and knew that counseling had helped her learn to manage many of the stressful situations she was currently experiencing as well as painful past experiences that continued to haunt her. She told her beloved that he should get counseling, too, because he very much needed it.

He adamantly responded that he did not need counseling. Besides, he told her, he'd never be able to trust a therapist to keep his most sensitive confidences.

The couple was heatedly arguing right in front of me at the conclusion of an otherwise pleasant social event. I didn't know what had triggered their conversation at this particular moment, but I listened to them without interruption.

Finally, the woman turned to me and asked my opinion. It was apparent that she wanted me to endorse her position. If I agreed with her, her argument would carry greater weight, particularly since I knew her guy very well and was myself a practicing psychologist.

Of course, instead of endorsing her position and alienating her significant other, I practiced open listening instead. I looked straight at her guy and asked him if he felt he needed therapy. Then I listened, aware of the frustration in his tone and body language, both of which revealed a great deal of resistance.

When he answered me, he said he was tired of his partner's constant pleas to start therapy. I asked him why he thought his partner pressed him so hard, and he said, "Because she loves me and wants me to rid myself of some of the most painful experiences in my life."

I made eye contact with him as I asked a timely follow-up question. "You seem conflicted about therapy because you are aware of painful things in your life that have scared you deeply. Is that how you feel?"

Quietly, he said it was true, adding, "I have demons, and they hurt a lot."

His girlfriend was paying close attention and appeared to be very much engaged by the effective non-judgmental listening she saw hard at work!

Finally, I shared my thoughts. I told the couple that therapy doesn't work unless the client is open to it. I also acknowledged that, unfortunately, some therapists are terrific and others are not, which makes seeking therapy a big decision. I also noted that therapy offered an opportunity for personal growth that could be life changing.

Once I was sure both partners were listening, I explained that they both had a stake in this important decision. I told them that seeing them openly listen to one another instead of arguing about therapy made me confident they would learn more about each other. In turn, this made me confident that their love would continue to grow no matter what they decided to do.

I offered a bit of advice just before I left. I said, "Try to learn what 'stakes' both of you have in this important decision because it affects both of you." I then told them I felt sure they would make the right decision and took my leave.

I know for a fact that this couple was able to address their collective and individual demons and go on to share a happy and supportive life together. Active listening is what enabled them to do this.

Active listening plays a big role in success in the workplace, too. I was once asked to coach a woman who worked in marketing. She had a reputation for being difficult to communicate with, close minded, and very defensive. When I first met her, I asked if her company reputation was a surprise to her. She responded quickly and directly, saying, "I hate working here, and I have a transfer request in to another department." She said she thought the other department would give her a "fresh start" to demonstrate her skills and help her earn a better reputation.

I asked an open-ended question that I hoped would be thought provoking. I said, "Help me understand the 'better reputation' you hope to make."

She responded that she hoped to be recognized as a smart person who was willing to go the extra mile to tackle tough challenges and meet obstacles head-on.

I asked a follow-up question meant to help her do some critical thinking. "Do you see yourself as having tackled some difficult obstacles successfully in your current job?"

She started to cry as she said, "They block me at every turn, and that really pisses me off."

This admission gave me the opportunity to provide personal counseling, and I seized the opportunity.

I said, "I can imagine how that would make you feel… Misunderstood at every turn?"

She nodded and eventually stopped crying as we exchanged ideas about her reactions when she was treated this way. I asked if she would work with me to replace her negative reactions—impatience and anger—with more positive ones like calming herself and even using some new approaches to communicate with her co-workers, including the listening skills in this chapter.

That was the beginning of a successful coaching relationship that lasted six months. Slowly and cautiously, she began to try new approaches including active listening, stress reduction, and eventually teamwork skills. For example, she learned to anticipate co-workers who resisted her at every turn as well as those who were not quite as difficult to work with. She began to selectively practice her new listening skills with those "easier" individuals. She mentally rehearsed how she wanted to interact with them, and when the opportunity came, she paid particular attention to their reactions to her and eased up or changed her demeanor accordingly. She mindfully worked not to take offense or communicate anger or impatience, and she looked for opportunities to show that she respected her co-workers and wanted to understand their resistance to her. She also practiced deep breathing before she engaged these individuals to help her stay calm.

She was by no means perfect, but as time went by, her co-workers became more receptive to her. The day a co-worker asked her advice on an area of her expertise, my client felt needed and valued for the first time in a long time, and I celebrated with her.

Her transfer suddenly came through, and just before she changed positions, she told me with confidence that she realized her new skills would make her new job a very different experience than her current one. She would be more effective because she now knew how to avoid alienating her co-workers. She was going to start her new job with a reborn sense of optimism that felt right to her.

Active listening, once again, made all the difference, yet experts find that most of us only hear 25%–50% of what we're told[18]. That means we pay attention to less than half the conversation! We would all benefit from paying closer attention to the many rich opportunities to listen in our daily lives. For instance:

- We can listen for information (particularly at school).
- We can listen to understand (particularly with friends and family).
- We can listen for enjoyment (particularly playing computer and video games and watching TV and good movies).
- We can listen to learn (particularly from respected teachers, good mentors, supervisors, and parents).

Try this resourceful idea: spend an entire dedicated day listening in *all* these life venues. Make it a goal to listen to everything. Focus completely on what is said to you. By the end of the day, you will be exhausted, but

---

18. "Active Listening," *Mind Tools*, 2018, https://www.mindtools.com/CommSkll/ActiveListening.htm.

hopefully you will also have a renewed appreciation of the value of listening in your everyday life. The old saying "listen and learn" is very apt indeed.

If you can hone this skill called active listening over your lifetime, whether personally, professionally, or, hopefully, both, it will pay off many times over.

In sum, here are my wisdoms for practicing the art of active listening:

- Just because you can listen doesn't mean you're good at listening. Active listening is a powerful tool you can use time and time again. Get talented at using this skill, and you will greatly increase the odds of success in your career and life.

- Every message has two parts—the content or substance of what is said and the tone or delivery of the message. On average, 80% of all communication is revealed in the tone of the message. That's good, because just listening for substance is tiring. People are much more motivated and enriched by experiencing tones while communicating with others. Great actors know this!

- Tones are conveyed through body language, facial expressions, and feelings and attitudes. The range of tones is almost infinite and can change in a heartbeat.

- The art of listening requires a complete understanding of substance and tones that are conveyed simultaneously. That's why listening is difficult for so many people. Very effective leaders perfect this skill to an art form.

- The best listeners are non-judgmental. They have an uncanny ability to keep their opinions from interfering with the help they offer. Most people can solve their own problems. When they identify their own solutions, their commitment to implementing them is often much greater than when solutions are given to them.

- You might or might not learn from the advice you receive. The temptation is usually to listen to it anyway, just in case it's useful. Just beware of people who take others' advice too quickly or totally reject it. In either case, they probably want to avoid taking responsibility for solving their problems.

- Listening to yourself as you seek the counsel of a non-evaluative listener isn't easy, but it's a great way to learn self-discovery and wisdom. It's the epitome of listening because you are listening to your own internal messages as well as to what others are saying to you.

Recommended Readings

Internet References

"Active Listening." *Mind Tools*, 2018. https://www.mindtools.com/CommSkll/ActiveListening.htm.

Frost, Shelley. "How to Listen without Judging." *Our Everyday Life*, March 15, 2018. https://oureverydaylife.com/listen-judging-11954.html.

Grohol, John M. "Become a Better Listener: Active Listening." *Psych Central*, 2018. https://psychcentral.com/lib/become-a-better-listener-active-listening/.

"Non-Verbal Communication." *Skills You Need*, 2018. https://www.skillsyouneed.com/ips/nonverbal-communication.html.

Chapter 9:

Lasting Friendships

THROUGHOUT YOUR LIFE, you will likely develop relationships with all kinds of people. As a young child, you probably spent time with other small playmates. When you began school, you no doubt made some new friends. As you grew older, you probably joined a few teams or clubs.

Most people feel the need to belong and be accepted, but meeting these needs isn't always easy. As you might already know, friends come and go. I remember my childhood playmates, but none of them became lifelong friends.

The psychologist Adam Grant recently surveyed seventh graders about their friendships. Because they're growing up in the Facebook era, many of them have Internet friends. In addition, they're accustomed to texting one another on their cell phones rather than making phone calls and engaging in conversations. Dr. Grant found that with the boundaries of friendship changing, many middle schoolers now struggle to determine who in fact is a "real friend"[19].

---

19. Adam Grant, "Do You Know Who Your Real Friends Are?" *Psychology Today*, July 31, 2014, https://www.psychologytoday.com/us/blog/give-and-take/201407/do-you-know-who-your-real-friends-are.

Be careful! Friends on the Internet might include people you've never met who might not be who they claim to be. Social media sites or apps such as Facebook, Instagram, and all kinds of computer and video games enable individuals to misrepresent themselves. You could meet someone who lies about their age or someone who claims to live near you who actually lives halfway around the world.

To further complicate things, researchers have found that about half of all adolescent friendships don't last to the next school year. What's more, a recent study of middle school students revealed that only 1% of friends lasted through high school.[20] The friendships that lasted the longest involved teens with similar genders, academic abilities, degrees of aggressiveness, and social status. The study also showed that girls are more likely to enjoy lasting school friendships than boys.

What exactly defines a good friend, given that friends and friendships change so much? Good friends talk often and hang out together. Good friends watch out for one another. They do each other favors, but they don't keep score or expect anything in return. They also share confidences with one another and offer constructive advice, personal feedback, and kindness. Bonds further increase when good friends share memories and experiences.

It's easy to separate friends into three groups: passing acquaintances, good friends, and best friends. In fact, as your friends get to know one another, they often introduce you to other people and your circle gets larger. Some teens become popular this way, but being popular comes with downsides as well as benefits. Popularity ensures a great social life but sometimes at the expense of schoolwork or other relationships. Friends can be greedy, especially if they are immature and expect your undivided attention.

Unfortunately, some people will disappoint you and even stab you in the back. When I was a university professor, I became good friends with

---

20. Tanaz Ahmed, "Study: Your Middle School Friendships Were Bound to Fail," *USA Today College*, August 20, 2015, http://college.usatoday.com/2015/08/20/study-middle-school-friendships-bound-to-fail/.

a student in my graduate class. I ended up mentoring him and eventually hiring him to work in my consulting company. Eventually, we began seeing one another socially. As we grew closer, we shared our most personal feelings and relied on one another for advice. When he began coaching the head of a major department for my company, the two men really hit it off, so much so that my close friend decided to break away and start his own business coaching the department head and all his managers. He knew this violated the agreement he'd made upon joining my firm, but the lucrative work and adulation from his new client were too tempting to resist.

I was really surprised my close friend would behave so unprofessionally. He still wanted to be my friend and told me so, but I broke off the relationship. This unfortunate experience taught me that I need my close friends to be ethical. I also learned that mixing business with pleasure isn't a good idea. I never again allowed myself to become close friends with people who worked for me. If I really liked them, I only pursued the friendship after we no longer worked together.

Friends can hurt you in other ways, too. Maybe you have friends who take advantage of you. They might use you to make new friends, borrow money from you that they don't intend to pay back, ask for answers on a test or homework, or take credit for work you did. They might worm their way into meetings you have with top managers they want to meet. Of course, none of these people are actually real friends, but getting blindsided by them is pretty common.

How can you deal with users? In your social life, it's often possible to avoid seeing them, but if they're in a social group with you such as a fraternity or sorority, you cannot entirely cut them off. Try your best to avoid doing special favors for them. Be upfront and privately tell them you're offended that they've used you. They will probably deny it or even say you're imagining things, but don't fall for it. Even if you want to keep their friendship, don't do them special favors anymore. Remember, friendship is a two-way street. If you find yourself giving more than you're getting, it might be time to change the friendship or put the person further outside your circle.

Friends who are co-workers can be helpful in several ways. A source of enjoyment, learning, and collaboration, they can help you get to know the ropes in a new job and keep you up to date on developments. Things can change, however, if you get a big promotion and become their boss. You can turn down the position or ask for a different one, but if your company wants you to take the job, you're stuck!

If this happens, you will be challenged to set clear boundaries because your first allegiance must be to your company. This situation will test your people sensitivity and your communication skills. The best managers anticipate how their former friends/coworkers will feel and meet with each individual privately to explain how they will manage them. Often, a full meeting with everyone in the department is held, and sometimes a facilitator is on hand to jumpstart conversations.

Happily, friendships often lead to lifelong relationships. If you're fortunate enough to have a few best friends in your adult life, count yourself very fortunate indeed. These individuals have probably been in your inner circle for some time. When you're young, you might have no shortage of best friends, but as you get older, you will be more discerning as you gain greater wisdom about yourself.

Life coaches consistently note certain ways best friends behave[21]. The more your close friends fit the following description, the more they qualify as candidates to be "best friends":

- Best friends are emotionally supportive through thick and thin; they pull you up when you need it most.

- Best friends bring out your best qualities and understand and accept you for who you are.

- Best friends listen without judgment; they have the unique ability to truly understand how you feel even if your words cannot quite express it.

---

21. "15 Traits of a High-Quality Best Friend," *Lifehack*, https://www.lifehack.org/articles/communication/15-traits-high-quality-best-friend.html.

- Best friends are there when you need them and go out of their way for you.
- Best friends are comfortable with you as soon as they meet you. Even if you don't see each other for some time, you pick up where you left off.
- Best friends' strong trust in you mirrors your trust in them; it is reciprocal, mutual, and enduring for you both.
- Best friends do things for you that no one else would think of; their thoughtfulness and caring are qualities you admire.
- Best friends are reliable and loyal and will watch out for you even when you don't ask them to.

Many happily married couples and life partners consider themselves best friends. Those who don't probably have shaky partnerships. When you think about finding the special love of your life, consider how that person has to pass through all the circles of your social map. That person is first an acquaintance, then a friend, and finally a close friend. Even if the person becomes a best friend, it's up to you to choose the special someone you are ready to love with all your heart.

Friends often say they love one another, and there are indeed many different kinds of love. When you love someone so much that you want to spend your life with this person, you might have found your "true love." You will no doubt have very warm feelings about this person who meets so many of your needs, but there is no magic formula. One couple I knew loved various brands of coffees and talked endlessly about savoring them together. This was the special glue that brought and held them together.

Of course, many adults remain single their entire lives and are perfectly happy. After losing my "best friend," my late wife, I enjoyed being single for a few years. Friends and family filled my life and I enjoyed meeting new people. Then, my loving daughter met my new special someone and praised her highly. She was right, at least initially. We dated, travelled together, and even began living with one another part of the year. Life was good the first few years until I began to get increasingly uncomfortable in our growing relationship. We parted company eventually, and I felt immediate relief. Remember, life itself is a chance, and taking chances is part of life.

In addition, thanks to longer life expectancies, many of us will develop and maintain many friends. Hopefully, your friends later in life will be richly diverse. Unfortunately, you will also lose very good friends as you age.

Many life circumstances cause us to lose dear friends. Some friends move far away, some relocate for better jobs, some friendships end abruptly and angrily, and perhaps the most traumatic is when a friend dies unexpectedly. My grandson recently lost a dear friend who took his own life. This was a complete surprise to my grandson and all his other friends, as well. My daughter was a high school student when four of her friends lost their lives in a tragic boating accident.

Here are some suggestions for coping with the great anguish caused by the loss of a treasured friend:

- Give yourself permission to grieve. You can grieve alone or with others. It makes no difference how you choose to grieve; just do it. Crying, sadness, and remorse are normal, and there is no set length of time that's appropriate when grieving. Your brain needs to heal, and we all heal in our own time and way.

- Try changing your mindset by asking yourself what you most enjoyed about your friend. Make a promise to think of this individual's great qualities as gifts you always get to cherish. In other words, gradually replace your painful thoughts with positive memories. This might bring you very emotionally close to your friend even though he or she is gone.

- If your loss is caused by a geographical move or relocation, keep in mind that geography doesn't have to signal the end of a friendship. You can connect in so many ways today. Cell phones and videoconferencing are possible virtually everywhere on the globe. Distance need not be an insurmountable barrier.

- If your friend is lost forever, you will need to practice patience to honor the friendship that once was. All friendships have rich histories and enrich our lives in different ways. While there might be great loss, be mindful that at least you had the benefit of a great friendship. During this time of sadness and healing, try to reach out to other friends for support. Make a special effort to stay close to these friends but also consider making new friends.

On a more uplifting note, human development specialist Karen Fingerman says that our friendships do get better as we age. In fact, older people are generally more happy and less judgmental than younger people. They are less driven by hormones and emotions, and they control themselves better. If you are fortunate, you will have some great friends in your lifetime.

Here are my wisdoms regarding friendships:

- At different stages of life, it's a good idea to step back and look at the people who are part of your social circle. Identify your best friends, good friends, and acquaintances. Your circle of friends might even help you decide who you want to get to know better and who you don't.

- It's up to you to change your relationships. Adults do it all the time in order to improve the quality of their lives and make room for new friends.

- When you're an adolescent, you will likely have many friends. By the time you finish high school, only about 1% of these friends will still be around. However, some school buddies will become lifelong friends. Just be sure your friends are real! Watch out for Internet friends you've never met.

- Being a friend makes you vulnerable. You gain enjoyment from friends, but some friends will hurt, disappoint, or even take advantage of you. This can feel unbearable, and it's up to you to get out of these relationships. If you don't know how to break up with these people, ask for help from someone you trust. If you find yourself stuck in a relationship with someone who hurts you, you might need to see a professional therapist for help.

- If you have friends who are dishonest or unethical, be very careful.

They likely assume their undesirable actions aren't important. If you prize your friendships, drop these people as soon as you can. If you have to work with them, be very vigilant and try to avoid getting involved in their deceit. Some executives have gone to prison because they lost objectivity around these cunning people.

- You likely will have a very few best friends in life. These special people will satisfy many personal needs. When several of your needs are satisfied together, your feelings of joy and happiness will multiply.

- Selecting your true love to join you on your lifelong journey will impact your entire life. In all likelihood, you will fall in love with a best friend. It's important to know yourself well enough to know what needs are most important to you. This is especially important when seeking true love.

Recommended Readings

Internet References

"15 Traits of a High-Quality Best Friend." *Lifehack*. https://www.lifehack.org/articles/communication/15-traits-high-quality-best-friend.html.

Ahmed, Tanaz. "Study: Your Middle School Friendships Were Bound to Fail." *USA Today College*, August 20, 2015. http://college.usatoday.com/2015/08/20/study-middle-school-friendships-bound-to-fail/.

Duffey, Thelma. "When You Lose a Friend." *Psychology Today*, April 27, 2015. https://www.psychologytoday.com/us/blog/works-in-progress/201504/when-you-lose-friend.

Grant, Adam. "Do You Know Who Your Real Friends Are?" *Psychology Today*, July 31, 2014. https://www.psychologytoday.com/us/blog/give-and-take/201407/do-you-know-who-your-real-friends-are.

Riggio, Ronald E. "4 Reasons Best Friends Stick Together (or Come Apart)." *Psychology Today*, July 31, 2015. https://www.psychologytoday.com/us/blog/cutting-edge-leadership/201507/4-reasons-best-friends-stick-together-or-come-apart.

Chapter 10:

Healthy Romantic Relationships

OUR CULTURE BOMBARDS us with messages about love. Novels and movies are replete with romantic love stories, and turning on the radio in the hopes of hearing a song that isn't about love is an exercise in futility. As if that's not enough, TV programs and commercials use love and relationships to attract viewers. Love is a big seller everywhere we go because our brains need love, we all seek love, and we admire and envy those who are deeply in love.

Finding lasting love is about as complex as it gets. Dating is scary because you don't yet know this person. It's a process of self-discovery as much as it's an opportunity to learn about the other person. My advice is to just be yourself. Don't try to be something or someone you're not. Have fun dating and getting to know many different people. Nothing says you have to find "the one" soon. Teens tend to pair up early in part because dating is fraught with anxiety and risk. Many think it's better to be in a secure relationship than to be "out there" on their own. After all, they can always break up if they change their minds.

I suppose that thinking is reasonable, but I've also known couples that dated exclusively all through college and then broke up soon after graduation. Those poor souls missed lots of dating opportunities while in college!

Give yourself plenty of time to date different people and narrow down the kind of person who's right for you. There are no hard and fast rules. Dating is a process of discovering what you want and need in another person. It's part of acquiring wisdom about yourself.

When you date, physical attraction and chemistry will draw you to certain individuals. Hormones are at work, and the thrill of the first kiss with someone special is undeniable, but that doesn't mean you have to jump into a relationship and run off to Vegas to get married!

Make your special someone your best friend first. Let your thinking brain kick in. Serious relationships aren't based on impulse. Before you spend every waking moment with your new love and jump into the sack to seal the deal, slow down! Give the relationship time to grow.

Here are several dating cautions that numerous relationship counselors[22] recommend:

- Don't waste time pondering whether or not someone might be "the one" for the first few months. Just relax, enjoy each date, and focus on having fun. Keep your expectations realistic, even when it's hard to do.

- Figure out how emotionally compatible you are before becoming intimate. Ask yourself if you're comfortable with your own sexuality and ready for sex. If you're uncomfortable, stop and give yourself more space. Your partner might want more from you, but proceed at a pace that makes sense to you. If your partner doesn't respect your choice, you have the wrong partner. Better to move on than have someone try to manipulate you into doing something you don't want to do or aren't ready for.

- If you choose to be intimate, use sex to explore your bodies together. Sexual contact is very important for closeness and communicating your feelings, but don't rush into intercourse or it will feel perfuncto-

---

22. Jill P. Weber, "5 Steps to Take before Starting a New Relationship," *Psychology Today*, July 17, 2013, https://www.psychologytoday.com/us/blog/having-sex-wanting-intimacy/201307/5-steps-take-starting-new-relationship.

ry rather than special. Most importantly, keep the lovemaking going even after sex. Sometimes lovers don't have a great first experience together. Remember, it takes time to learn what satisfies you both. And be sure to use protection every time unless you both want to get pregnant.

- Your family should not meet your special someone for at least a month or two. Keep dating and make sure there are no "red flags." If red flags appear, decide whether you want to keep dating, break things off, or slow down and start dating other people. No matter what you decide, keep your family out of it until you feel the person is right for you. Casual dates and family seldom mix.

- Use "self-talk" if a dating relationship begins to feel rushed, awkward, or uncomfortable. In other words, listen to yourself. This is a critical part of understanding yourself and using your wisdom. If your "self-talk" goes the other way, the more you see this person, the happier you'll be. You'll daydream about your special someone, miss this person when you're not together, and feel energized and excited thinking about upcoming dates.

- Focus on whether you like your partner rather than on whether your partner likes you. If you are plagued by nagging doubts, call things off and move on. Don't naively think your partner will mature or outgrow behaviors that make you uncomfortable. Better to devote your energy to meeting someone else.

Clinical psychologist Jill P. Weber offers excellent advice for dating[23]. Above all, she cautions women to take it seriously if they sense "He's just not

---

23. Jill P. Weber, "5 Steps to Take before Starting a New Relationship," *Psychology Today*, July 17, 2013, https://www.psychologytoday.com/us/blog/having-sex-wanting-intimacy/201307/5-steps-take-starting-new-relationship.

into you." The same goes for men. She also cautions women against trying to change themselves to be "the perfect match for Mr. [or Ms.] right."

I couldn't agree more. You shouldn't try to entice another person to be attracted to you. It isn't fair to you and it doesn't work anyway. Better to devote yourself to your own development. If you're shy, learn how to compensate. If you're introverted, seek out other people in small groups or alone. If others perceive you as drab or uninteresting, work on your persona and dress. Develop new interests you enjoy and work to meet other people with similar interests.

Here are Dr. Webber's principles for finding the right match:

- Understand yourself sexually and emotionally. If you harbor the unrealistic hope that someone else will understand you and make you happy, you need to reverse your thinking. It's up to you to tell the other person about your emotions and sexual desires rather than hoping your partner will intuitively perceive your needs. You are your own person. You do not need to always please someone else to be in a committed relationship.

- Believe what people say about themselves. If a date says he doesn't want a serious relationship but you do, move on. Don't kid yourself into thinking he'll change his mind after he knows you better. If a date says he does want a serious relationship but you don't, also move on. You need to be on the same page. In college, I dated a number of women. I always told them I was going to graduate school and didn't want a serious relationship. I thought maybe women wouldn't want to date me, but that was far from the case. Plenty of women felt the same way, including my future wife. We dated on and off in college, got engaged in grad school, and married a year later.

- Avoid "sextimacy." If you think hastening a sexual relationship will lead to emotional intimacy and a committed relationship, think again. Researchers have found that having sex before emotional intimacy exists does not lead to committed partnerships. Better to work on finding a person who will like you for yourself. Sex should be an expression of love as a relationship deepens.

- Separate yourself psychologically from your parents. This is no easy thing to do. It starts gradually and can take a lifetime. To form healthy relationships with a partner, you have to be ready to meet your emotional needs with that partner. If you depend on your parents for emotional support or to make life decisions, it will be a challenge to live independently, much less live with a committed partner. It's not uncommon to see marriages break apart because of interfering parents. Healthy families produce independent children who are ready for adulthood. If you enter a partnership thinking your loved one will take care of you the same way your parents did, watch out. This expectation can breed resentment, anger, and even competition for your affection from your partner.

- Put yourself in new situations. If you've experienced failed relationships, you might want to withdraw from dating for a while and "work on" yourself. However, that approach is more like hiding and leads to loneliness, sadness, and loss. Better to keep dating, explore new relationships, and focus on what you need in a partner that's different from what you had before. You don't want to repeat your mistakes. Accept your blind spots and move on. Each new dating experience is a unique opportunity that can afford up-to-the-moment awareness of your preferences, strengths, and weaknesses. Deliberately put yourself in new and novel situations, and you just might meet your special someone.

Meeting people is a prerequisite for dating. Highly social people who enjoy new friendships have an advantage, but what about shy people? I don't suggest that shy people embark on a personality remake. However, following a few tips can help these individuals more easily engage in conversation and meet new people[24].

---

24. Erika Casriel, "Shedding Shyness," *Psychology Today*, March 1, 2007, https://www.psychologytoday.com/us/articles/200703/shedding-shyness.

If you're going to a party, arrive early and meet others one on one. As more people come in, talk to them for short periods. Don't put a lot of pressure on yourself in your initial swing through the crowd. You don't need to meet everyone. Just go back to the people who interest you and make an effort to be a good listener. You don't need to say anything brilliant, nor do you need to be an expert. Above all, refrain from judging what people say to you. Add comments and ideas as you listen to others. People like good listeners.

To make a good first impression, maintain a relaxed position and lean slightly forward as you make eye contact. Soften your gaze by moving your eyes slightly around the other person's face. Say something about the environment such as, "The traffic was murder on the way here." You don't need to be entertaining. People often think they need to be witty or sophisticated. What they need is simply to be nice.

You can also give extra information when responding to others, such as, "You lived in Queens, too? I went to some great concerts and tennis matches there when I was growing up." Such a response gives other people running room to respond. You don't need to have a deep conversation to get the ball rolling, but don't just walk away if there's a lull. Summarize your thoughts if they're relevant or try asking a pregnant question to spark new conversation. Let's say the conversation is about tough parking rules on campus. You might say something like, "I wonder what's going on with parking permits. So many spots aren't being used. Why is that?"

A few tips for flirting: adopt a carefree attitude. Crack a joke. Do something a bit silly but fun. Smile when someone is nice to you. Laugh easily if you're having a good time. Be agreeable. Everyone prefers to hear "you're right" rather than "you're wrong," and research shows that people who agree with others are perceived as more intelligent. Of course, don't simply agree with everything that's said. People also want to know why you agree with them. Remember when you were a child and gave a coy smile to attract loving attention? Facial expressions are one of the best ways to express natural flirtatiousness.

Until you find your true love, enjoy the many different types of love that human beings experience. According to psychologist Robert Sternberg[25], these include:

- Liking. This characterizes close friendships, particularly best friends, and includes feelings of bonding, warmth, and closeness with another person but not intense passion or long-term commitment. I had a couple of close friends growing up, but we lost touch as life progressed. On the other hand, sometimes childhood friends last a lifetime.

- Infatuation. This is often called "love at first sight." The passion is there, but it can suddenly disappear because there's no intimacy or commitment. Teens sometimes become infatuated with their favorite stars or with a high school or college athlete or someone else who's in the limelight.

- Empty love. Sometimes strong love deteriorates. The commitment is still there but not the passion or intimacy. In some marriages, people stay married for the sake of the children. This is sad but true.

- Romantic love. This is the Hollywood version of love in which romantic lovers bond through passion and arousal. A whirlwind romance takes place and then evaporates.

- Companion love. This occurs in long-term relationships when the passion is gone but deep affection and commitment remain. Some people spend a lifetime with their partners without any physical desire for intimacy. This bond is stronger than friendship because of the extra component of commitment. Sometimes people live together for many years in this kind of relationship.

---

25. R. J. Sternberg, "A Triangular Theory of Love," *Psychological Review*, 1986, 93, 119–135.

- Fatuous love. This happens when people have a whirlwind courtship and then marry. Their commitment is largely determined by their passion for one another, but there's no intimacy to secure the relationship.

- Consummate love. This is the ideal kind of love, and it consists of three distinct components: intimacy, passion, and commitment. Dr. Sternberg cautions that maintaining consummate love might be harder than achieving it. Great love of this kind takes renewal and growth. The relationship requires complete dedication to making each other happy, being there in times of need, experimenting with sex and playfulness, and growing into an ever deeper level of affection.

Is it possible to remain madly in love with someone you've been with five, 10, or even 20 years? Two researchers took MRI brain scans of happily married individuals who reported intense romantic love for their partners an average of 21 years after they were married[26]. Neural activity was much higher for these couples in a dopamine-rich area of the brain, the VTA (ventral tegmental area).

The researchers concluded that intense romantic love consists of motivated behaviors. There is a craving for the union and focused attention and energy devoted to the partner, a strong desire to make the partner happy, and sexual attraction and thinking about the partner when apart.

Another landmark study comparing the brain scans of couples who recently fell in love with those of couples in intense, long-term romantic relationships found remarkable similarities. The researchers concluded that consummate love can last but that it takes hard work because love isn't

---

26. "Love and the Brain," Department of Neurobiology, *Harvard Medical School*, 2018, http://neuro.hms.harvard.edu/harvard-mahoney-neuroscience-institute/brain-newsletter/and-brain-series/love-and-brain.

static. People change and so does love, but loving partners can grow closer together. The dopamine-rich brain centers control motivation and the desire to unite and remain close in long-term relationships. The rewards of such relationships typically include a reduction in stress and increased feelings of security and calmness[27].

I suspect that similar studies comparing single and married people might explain the finding that, on average, married people are happier and live longer. There are many happy and healthy singles, but married couples that maintain consummate love experience all that love—and life—has to offer. Nonetheless, the research is far from conclusive and more carefully controlled studies are needed.

In sum, here are my wisdoms on healthy romantic relationships:

- Finding your special love is complex. It's as much about self-discovery as it is about discovering a special partner. You will learn about your preferences and what your personal needs are as you search for that special someone. In my opinion, it's ideal to seek a best friend who makes you feel special and loved.

- Dating is scary, fraught with uncertainties and possible rejection. Just try to be yourself and give yourself plenty of time. In other words, don't rush into relationships. Love at first sight might be how you feel, but it takes patience, caring, and exploration for relationships to blossom. Serious relationships don't develop on impulse. Every relationship is an opportunity to increase wisdom and self-understanding, even ones that go nowhere or end in pain.

- When dating, exercise the "cautions" I gave you all along the journey. Give yourself ample opportunity for self-talk as relationships grow closer. Above all, proceed at a pace that feels comfortable and right

---

27. Linda Geddes, "Couples Are Healthier, Wealthier…and Less Trim," *The Guardian*, April 17, 2016, https://www.theguardian.com/lifeandstyle/2016/apr/17/couples-healthier-wealthier-marriage-good-health-single-survey-research.

for you. Don't naively think your partner will change to suit you or that you will change to suit your partner. Pleasing one another should come naturally for both of you. If you sense red flags, face them and honestly decide if you want to accept them in your relationship. Better to step out of a relationship than endure one that's not right for you.

- Passion, intimacy, and commitment are the building blocks of true love. Couples that are deeply in love experience all three qualities, but it takes a great deal of effort and renewal to keep the fire burning. Couples can reach consummate love and maintain it for a lifetime, but love isn't static; it keeps changing.

- Loving couples are synergistic; they experiment, explore, and learn from one another to keep love alive. Couples can reignite love if the flames die down, but it takes honesty, openness, and a great deal of communication to do so.

- Love is a creation between partners. At its best, it's the greatest gift each partner can give the other.

Recommended Readings

Internet References

Casriel, Erika. "Shedding Shyness." *Psychology Today*, March 1, 2007. https://www.psychologytoday.com/us/articles/200703/shedding-shyness.

Geddes, Linda. "Couples Are Healthier, Wealthier…and Less Trim." *The Guardian*, April 17, 2016. https://www.theguardian.com/lifeandstyle/2016/apr/17/couples-healthier-wealthier-marriage-good-health-single-survey-research.

"Love and the Brain." Department of Neurobiology, *Harvard Medical School*, 2018. http://neuro.hms.harvard.edu/harvard-mahoney-neuroscience-institute/brain-newsletter/and-brain-series/love-and-brain.

Weber, Jill P. "5 Steps to Take before Starting a New Relationship." *Psychology Today*, July 17, 2013. https://www.psychologytoday.com/us/blog/having-sex-wanting-intimacy/201307/5-steps-take-starting-new-relationship.

Whitbourne, Susan Krauss. "Which of the 7 Types of Love Relationships Fits Yours?" *Psychology Today*, August 17, 2013. https://www.psychologytoday.com/us/blog/fulfillment-any-age/201308/which-the-7-types-love-relationships-fits-yours.

Print References

Sternberg, R. J. "A Triangular Theory of Love." *Psychological Review*. 1986, 93, 119–135.

Chapter 11:

Stress Management

FROM TIME TO TIME, we all feel frustration, fear, sorrow, impatience, anger, guilt, and anguish. These negative emotions cause a psychological state called stress that can be your best friend or your worst enemy.

Teens in particular react quickly to stress, especially when they sense harm or threat. They haven't yet developed the mental restraint to think first. This is one reason teen violence, especially in gangs, is so serious. Watch the classic 1961 movie *West Side Story* to see teens in gangs stressing themselves to the point that their feelings spill over to rage and then to violence.

Under stress, men respond differently from women, often by using physical strength[28]. Some researchers suggest this is due to a gene that only men have. Women, on the other hand, are more likely to use their wits to try to defuse stressful situations or to seek out the support of good friends. Researchers have found that certain hormones in women, particularly oxytocin manufactured in the brain, might contribute to how women cope with stress.

It might sound counterintuitive, but sometimes stress is good. It can help you rev up for important meetings or exams, and in emergencies, it can even save your life. For example, when an airplane crashed into the Potomac River in the dead of winter, one man dove into the frigid ice water and rescued several passengers by himself. In another real-life case, a man lifted a car to save a young boy pinned under the wheels. Both men summoned extraordinary powers of endurance and physical strength that simply aren't possible except in moments of great stress.

But stress is sometimes bad, as when it causes stage fright that freezes men and women alike in their tracks. Stress can be especially damaging if you carry it around without realizing it. Psychologists call this "trait anxiety" because the tension doesn't go away; individuals with trait anxiety are always tense[29]. Sometimes their stress gets so high that relationships at school and work and with friends and family suffer. Trait anxiety left untreated can even cause serious mental or physical problems.

Another common kind of stress is "state anxiety" caused by particular situations in a specific moment. An argument with a friend is a good example,

---

28. Gail Gross, "How Men and Women Handle Stress Differently," *Huffington Post*, November 9, 2016, https://www.huffingtonpost.com/entry/how-men-and-women-handle-stress-differently_us_58236ec5e4b0334571e0a4cd.

29. Rudolph Hatfield, "Difference between State and Trait Anxiety," *Livestrong*, August 14, 2017, https://www.livestrong.com/article/98672-differences-between-state-anxiety-/.

as is getting a low grade on a test or a poor evaluation from a boss. Most times, the anxiety passes and we get over it quickly, but some individuals just can't let things go.

Most of the time our stress is real, but the brain makes no distinction between events that actually happen and those we mistakenly think have occurred. Have you ever been angry at someone for wronging you only to discover the perpetrator was someone else?

You can tell if stress is getting the best of you by learning to recognize common signs. Stress can cause irritability and even impatience with other people in ways that might surprise you. For example, you might yell at your brother after you have a bad day at school. You might unexpectedly snap at your spouse after your boss treats you unfairly at work. It's very important to recognize your stress triggers. We all have them. The ability to find adaptive ways of coping with stress is a sign of maturity, and three basic strategies exist: change the stress situations you face, change the way you think about and handle those situations, or make important changes to your life.

Basic Strategies for Stress Reduction

The first strategy is the easiest--change the stress situations you face. To do this, you must first identify your stress triggers. Perhaps very tense or argumentative people trigger you. Try to see these individuals less often, and, if possible, maybe avoid them entirely. If you're highly competitive and the pressure is getting to you, you might stop playing a competitive sport and pick up one that's more fun. If watching the nightly news triggers your stress and makes you unable to relax for the rest of the evening, stop watching and find another way to stay current.

Changing the way you think about stressful situations can also be effective. If someone insults you, for example, try rethinking the situation instead of taking it personally. Maybe the person is thoughtless. If you expect this behavior, you might be able to train yourself to deflect thoughtless remarks or even shrug them off.

That said, it's not easy to change the way you think, especially if you have a lot of negative thoughts or tend to worry about failure. If this describes you, it might well be time to learn how to replace your anxious thoughts with healthier ones. For example, if you find yourself saying "I can't" a lot, try to replace this destructive message with a more positive one. Maybe you could say, "I don't know how yet, but I can learn," or, "I can do it if I just take a baby step or two first and inch along until I get the hang of it."

The second strategy for coping with stressful situations is to challenge yourself to be resourceful by changing the way you think about and handle such situations. Try counting your blessings, trying new activities, finding ways to use your positive qualities, enjoying your friends, or making new ones. Laughter is a great way to reduce stress, so deliberately seek funny movies and jokes that cause you to laugh deep from the belly.

Granted, changing your thinking can be tough, especially if you're under a lot of stress. If you think you need professional help, talk to your doctor. Everyone needs help sometimes. It's a sign of maturity to ask for help and accept it. A trusted counselor can help you learn kinder and more constructive ways of thinking about yourself.

The third and most challenging stress-reduction strategy involves changing your life. If you find yourself in a dead-end job or marriage that's causing great distress, you have to accept the sober fact that you face a fork in the road. Your life must take a new course, and you probably know it. Wisdom requires you to step out of yourself long enough to consider leaving this life behind and starting a new one.

This usually means making great sacrifices because it's seldom easy to make significant life changes. You might be held back by very real constraints. Just thinking about the dilemmas you face might cause even greater stress. For this reason, some people resign themselves to unsatisfactory lives and essentially give up. Psychologists call this strategy "learned helplessness," and it can be very self-destructive.

Don't give up on yourself, no matter what sacrifices you have to make, even if you have to totally reinvent your life. I was once asked to coach a manager with a lot of experience and talent whose work was slipping. She sometimes missed deadlines and had problems concentrating. Her boss talked to her, but she denied that anything was wrong. Eventually, she began to lose patience with some of her colleagues, blaming them for sloppy work she had to redo.

When I met her, I found her pleasant and cooperative. We talked about her work, and she said she could get on top of things and back to her old self if only her marriage were better. She had married late in life, and her husband was causing her a great deal of pain. He was verbally abusive, and she had grown to realize their marriage had been a mistake. He put her down constantly and blamed her for his misfortunes. She felt trapped and was losing sleep. Her job no longer challenged her, and she dreamed of the day she could retire, escape to the West Coast, and begin a new career in art, her first love.

Once she realized her problems stemmed from unhappiness and distress, she wanted my help constructing what she called her "exit plan." She consulted a divorce attorney and began addressing her finances and planning for the sale of her home. As she took these steps, she suddenly had more energy for her job. In time, her boss commended her work, which boosted her self-esteem. After a few years, she left both her marriage and her job. She now lives in a smaller, less expensive home out West, where she works as a curator in a small museum featuring Western art. As soon as she was in control of her life again, she found herself laughing more and having fun again.

The best way to avoid harmful stress is to recognize how your body handles it. All stress affects your body[30]. Here are the most common ways your body works to protect you when you face a crisis or severe life problem:

- Your muscles become tense.

- You either do not sleep or sleep fitfully.

---

30. Karen Frazier, "Physical Symptoms of Severe Stress," *Love to Know*, 2018, https://stress.lovetoknow.com/Physical_Symptoms_of_Severe_Stress.

- Your blood pressure rises.
- Your heart rate increases.
- Your digestive system slows down.
- Your immune system becomes compromised and you tend to get sick more often.
- Your breathing gets faster and shallower.
- Stress hormones such as cortisol and adrenaline kick in.

Not all of these reactions occur, nor do they all occur at once. Some are more gradual, and you might not even notice others until they become chronic. The symptoms can take virtually any form. Perhaps you have recurrent headaches or become tearful for no apparent reason. Know your body. When you experience symptoms that are unusual for you, it's time to consider that stress might be a factor.

Psychologists have identified three common responses when individuals become overwhelmed by stress[31]. The first is called the *fight response*. You get angry, agitated, overly emotional, and keyed up, with tension building quickly.

The second response is the *flight response*. You withdraw, pull away, shut down, space out, and experience depression. Or, conversely, you become apathetic and have no emotion at all.

The third response is the *crisis response*. Initially, you freeze under the extreme pressure. Your body can even become briefly paralyzed, but under the surface you are highly agitated and preparing to escape. If you do, your body collapses soon afterward.

I've only experienced one crisis response in my life, and I hope I never experience it again! I was driving on a scenic highway. The lane on my left had a steep embankment and heavy brush; my right lane had a beautiful bay

---

31. "Fight-or-Flight Reaction," *Changing Minds*, 2018, http://changingminds.org/explanations/brain/fight_flight.htm.

view with a steep drop into the water. On instinct, I swerved sharply to my left to avoid a collision with a large truck unexpectedly swerving right at me. As my car approached the embankment and I realized I was about to crash, I grabbed the wheel and spun it around. My car jackknifed and came to rest on both lanes. I realized I had to get off the road fast to avoid oncoming traffic, but I was paralyzed and couldn't move. My brain said, "Move fast!" but my body was frozen.

I sat in my car for what seemed an eternity but was probably no more than a few minutes before I managed to steer my car safely off the road. I was perspiring and shaken but otherwise unharmed. I was very lucky.

Crises come in different forms. Oftentimes, all we can do is hope for some warning and then implement an escape plan. Hurricanes are a good example, but auto accidents are another matter. They can happen extremely quickly and without notice. Always wear your seat belt. Had I not been wearing mine, I would have been thrown to the passenger side of my car. Frozen by my crisis response, I would not have been able to reach my steering wheel to drive off the road.

If you're experiencing a lot of stress, start managing and even reducing it. I suggest you learn what works best for you and that you keep this "stress toolbox" handy. My stress toolbox consists of the following relaxation techniques. I regularly:

- Watch beautiful sunsets just outside my door. Nature is a great relaxer after a stress-filled day.

- Use deep breathing. I inhale slowly and repeat a mantra such as "Relax" to myself, then close my eyes and breathe from my belly 5–10 times.

- Close my eyes gently and visualize great experiences I've had. For example, if I consciously recall the wonderful experience I had seeing an incredible lava flow from my Hawaiian cruise ship, my mood lifts.

- Watch my favorite hilarious movies, especially when I'm sad. Laughter actually changes the chemistry of the brain!

An underutilized solution for relieving stress is to pamper yourself. Here are some time-honored ways to do it:

- Breathe in the scent of lavender in your home. Lavender reduces the heart rate and blood pressure. It can help you relax and even fall asleep.
- Treat yourself to a chocolate-covered cherry or strawberry treat.
- Take a soothing bath. I like to take baths while listening to my favorite music. Sometimes I let my imagination wander to faraway places I've enjoyed. At other times, I close my eyes and let the music just soak in.
- Give yourself a scalp treatment while you close your eyes and sit back and just relax.
- Take a Swedish massage or a sauna. I find this calming and soothing, and it gets me in harmony with my body.
- Try yoga and meditation. Both are popular and affordable calming experiences.
- Give yourself a foot rub.

As many as 75% of all doctor's visits are believed to be caused by stress[32]. Stress affects people in different ways, but it contributes to illness regardless of gender[33]. Health researchers are just beginning to understand how chronic stress influences a wide range of diseases such as heart disease, high blood pressure, diabetes, and even early death. It's no exaggeration to say that stress is a national health problem.

In sum, here are my wisdoms for managing stress:

---

32. Elizabeth Agnvall, "Stress! Don't Let It Make You Sick," *AARP*, November 2014, https://www.aarp.org/health/healthy-living/info-2014/stress-and-disease.html.

33. Ibid.

- The brain makes no distinction between real and imagined stress. Your body reacts to both in exactly the same way.

- The brains of young people are still developing, which is why they have a greater tendency to overreact to threats and trying situations. It's especially important for them to identify and avoid stress triggers whenever they can. When they cannot, they need to have a toolbox ready with effective ways of reducing tension.

- It's easier to change the situations that cause stress than to change the way you react to stress. You might think you have little control over what stresses you, but if you're resourceful, you might surprise yourself. You cannot rid yourself entirely of situations that cause distress, but you can choose to modify them.

- We all have negative thoughts, and these thoughts cause stress. There is nothing you can do about events that have already happened. Stay in the present and concentrate on those situations you can reasonably change. If, despite your best efforts, you have to live with certain situations, try to modify your thoughts in order to calm yourself. Sometimes it helps to reduce your expectations before facing predictably upsetting or frustrating situations. If you know they will cause you stress, you might not be quite as upset when they do. Just remember to take care of yourself afterward.

- Stress can be your friend as well as your enemy. Sometimes stress prepares you to be more alert and strong in difficult situations. Some individuals even surprise themselves in times of crisis. You never know how you're going to perform. Do not underestimate yourself when times get tough.

- Laughter is great medicine for the brain. Laughing at yourself over something silly you said or did is far better than getting down on yourself. When you laugh, the chemistry in your brain changes for the better.

Barry M. Cohen, PhD

Recommended Readings

Internet References

Agnvall, Elizabeth. "Stress! Don't Let It Make You Sick." *AARP*, November 2014. https://www.aarp.org/health/healthy-living/info-2014/stress-and-disease.html.

Alvarez, Manny. "10 Ways to Relieve Stress Naturally." *Fox News*, December 24, 2013. http://www.foxnews.com/health/2012/01/27/10-ways-to-relieve-stress-naturally.html.

"Fight-or-Flight Reaction." *Changing Minds*, 2018. http://changingminds.org/explanations/brain/fight_flight.htm.

Frazier, Karen. "Physical Symptoms of Severe Stress." *Love to Know*, 2018. https://stress.lovetoknow.com/Physical_Symptoms_of_Severe_Stress.

Gross, Gail. "How Men and Women Handle Stress Differently." *Huffington Post*, November 9, 2016. https://www.huffingtonpost.com/entry/how-men-and-women-handle-stress-differently_us_58236ec5e4b0334571e0a4cd.

Hatfield, Rudolph. "Difference between State and Trait Anxiety." *Livestrong*, August 14, 2017. https://www.livestrong.com/article/98672-differences-between-state-anxiety-/.

Rinkunas, Susan. "Pamper Yourself! 8 Natural Stress Relievers." *Health*, March 6, 2014. http://www.health.com/mind-body/pamper-yourself-8-natural-stress-relievers#get-a-swedish-massage-0.

Chapter 12:

Resilience

Resilience is the ability to bounce back from painful setbacks or traumas. Sad to say, horrible life experiences come in many forms. I hope you never experience serious trauma, but even if you're lucky, you will inevitably experience a good taste of pain and frustration.

I'm not trying to scare you or discourage you from taking on life's great challenges. A life led so cautiously that you never put yourself in harm's way is both impossible and ill advised. You owe it to yourself to take intelligent risks and go for your dreams. Don't let pessimists discourage you. Just be resilient.

The personality quality most characteristic of resilient people is optimism[34]. Resilient people think positively about life and all it can offer. When they experience tragedy, they hurt just as much as anyone else, but they also begin thinking of new possibilities that will help them live, not just survive.

By contrast, people who cannot get past terrible experiences repeatedly think of their misfortunes. Their negative thoughts drag them down. In fact,

---

34. Harry Mills and Mark Dombeck, "Resilience: Optimism," *Gracepoint*, 2017, https://www.gracepointwellness.org/298-emotional-resilience/article/5789-resilience-optimism.

they often become depressed and listless. They might not sleep well, and they often withdraw from everyone, even their own families.

Psychologists know that having faith and/or a religious belief system can be a great source of comfort and strength, especially in the midst of terrible life experiences[35]. Those who are religious often gain support from others in their church—just think of natural disasters and how people seek the solace of their religious communities to get through these challenging times—but faith in and of itself is a source of courage and a means of reducing distress and fear.

Individuals facing trauma need the support of friends, neighbors, and loved ones. Sometimes complete strangers will band together for support when a crisis occurs. While the pessimist struggles and withdraws from people, the optimist is right there, problem solving. In an earlier chapter, I mentioned that groups can problem solve much better than the average person in a group[36]. When people work together, they form a team, and teams are very different from groups. If you're a member of a team tackling a crisis, my guess is you'll see leaders quickly emerge.

Winston Churchill said courage is the key ingredient that makes leadership possible. In a crisis, our best leaders often emerge from nowhere. This is because leadership talent can be dormant. Those leaders who emerge are resilient.

Psychologists say resilience is a process or series of behaviors that can be utilized over a lifetime of continual frustrating situations. I believe this is accurate. I was a caregiver for six years for my wife as she slowly wasted away from a degenerative disease with no treatment or cure called myotonic dystrophy. This was a very stressful time in my life. My wife accepted her

---

35. "The Road to Resilience," *American Psychological Association*, 2018, http://www.apa.org/helpcenter/road-resilience.aspx.

36. R. Large and R. K. White, "Experimental Study of Leadership and Group Life," *Readings in Social Psychology*, 1958.

fate and often said, "It is what it is." That was a mark of her maturity, and I admired her for living as fully as she could.

Regretfully, I wasn't nearly as resilient. I worried a lot about her falling because her disease would worsen if she were seriously hurt in a fall. I stayed home and took care of her and kept her as safe as possible. I had no idea I was becoming more and more of what our culture calls a "couch potato" while caring for my wife who could hardly walk. Good friends suggested I put her in a nursing home, but I couldn't. I knew my wife would stay with me right to the end, and I was going to stay with her right to the end.

About this time, I suffered a stroke. Where had this come from? My health was good and I had no cardiac or blood pressure problems. Fortunately, my stroke was minor and left me with no permanent damage. When I was recovering, my brother gave me some personal feedback that was hard to hear. He said I'd acted stupidly by insisting on taking care of my wife without any help. He also told me that, as a psychologist, I should have known better. Finally, he advised me to hire caregivers for my wife.

I took his advice. After hiring two terrific caregivers, I found myself rebounding. I was in control of my life again! Turns out, my stroke was caused by stress and anxiety and further compounded by a lack of physical activity. Indeed, doctors believe almost half of all medical conditions have psychological causes. I am a living example!

Psychologists also agree that resilience is not inherited[37]. We each have to develop it on our own. You can develop the ability to be resilient throughout life by:

- Calming yourself and thinking clearly during crises or very trying times

- Tolerating uncertainty and even unknown causes to threats you must handle

---

37. "Resilience: Build Skills to Endure Hardship," *Mayo Clinic*, 2018, https://www.mayoclinic.org/tests-procedures/resilience-training/in-depth/resilience/art-20046311.

- Having a healthy self-concept and confidence in yourself
- Being playful and able to laugh at yourself
- Being optimistic and believing tough times and other difficulties will pass
- Remaining resourceful while seeking new ways to solve difficult problems
- Making close friends and best buddies you can count on when you need them
- Adjusting to different personalities while remaining your own person
- Learning from experience and looking back realistically at your mistakes
- Solving problems whether working alone or with others

We all experience painful setbacks and trauma. The good news is, resilience can be mindfully developed. One challenge every human being faces is learning to be resilient when coping with people who cause you grief and even harm. While I hope most of your relationships will enhance your life, sadly, some likely won't.

A very disagreeable person isn't someone you merely dislike; it's someone who intentionally or unintentionally makes you uncomfortable or causes you pain or harm. This could be a friend, a co-worker, a boss, a neighbor, or even a family member.

Some individuals live in abusive relationships. Typically, one partner dominates the other, threatens physical harm, or physically attacks in uncontrollable rages. The controlling partner might also attack emotionally by making demeaning remarks and putting the other person down at every opportunity.

Regretfully, abused adults or children often do not know they are being abused until much later in life because the abuse feels normal. Without competent counsel or awareness of what is happening, the abuse goes on. The most telltale sign of an abusive relationship is fear of a partner or parent[38]. Abused individuals also experience self-loathing, helplessness, or desperation and feel like they are "walking on eggshells" around the abuser.

Most tragic is a young child who has been sexually abused or an abused spouse who feels powerless to escape, often because children are involved.

Sometimes abuse even results in death. If your safety is threatened, you must get out of the relationship. Physical abusers often ask forgiveness for their hurtful actions, but make no mistake, they will repeat it. They can't help themselves. Call upon your resilience to escape early and don't look back. The longer someone stays in an abusive relationship, the harder it is to get out and the more damaging it can be.

Keep in mind that it makes no difference why people abuse others. Perhaps it's because they were abused themselves or because they experienced unspeakable horror in military combat. The reason is irrelevant. The fact is, these people urgently need psychiatric treatment and counseling. Unfortunately, sometimes an abused partner unrealistically hangs on to the relationship in the belief that the abuser will somehow change. That is wishful thinking. It is an unproductive way of putting a Band-Aid on a sore that is festering and will only worsen.

Abuse occurs outside the family, too. As many as 20% of children are abused by bullies in school who sometimes demand favors in return for cutting back on their abuse[39]. Maybe they want your completed homework or for you to do their homework for them. Maybe they want money. Bullies often pick on those who are weaker than they are.

You cannot escape bullies. They will find you and corner you, and you must be resilient in order to learn how to deal with them. I began learning this when I was 10. I was at a summer resort when I met a boy my age who didn't have any friends. When school started, I realized this boy attended my

---

38. *Help Guide*, 2018, www.helpguide.org.

39. "Bullying Statistics," *Pacer's National Bullying Prevention Center*, 2018, http://www.pacer.org/bullying/resources/stats.asp.

school. He began to taunt me, call me names, and chase me on my way to school. I quickly realized I was being harassed and that the boy enjoyed it. Naturally, I was upset. Day after day, I took different routes to school in order to avoid him, but he always caught up with me and began to punch me. I was afraid to fight back for fear his bullying would intensify.

Finally, I told my dad what was happening. I suppose he should have asked my teachers and principal for help, but he said I had to learn to stand up for myself. My dad also said that if I physically fought this fellow, I could take him. I played sports and was stronger than the bully. To this day, I value my dad's confidence in me.

The day came for the showdown. My dad and some other kids watched me fight the bully. We smacked one another hard, and then I landed a punch right on the bully's nose. He fell down but got up. He landed a punch on me that hurt, but I didn't let it show. The bully then left, and most of the kids watching the fight patted me on my shoulder. That was the first time I realized the bully probably picked on other kids, too. It's funny–when you're being abused, you often think you're the only one.

The bully backed down for a while but continued to call me names. Finally, a friend of mine who was known as a "tough kid" in the neighborhood found out about the fight and asked me about the bully. After I explained what had happened, my friend approached the bully and told him if he ever heard he was picking on me again, he'd give him a beating he'd never forget.

That was the end of my terrible experience, but a word of caution—my dad's advice to fight back wouldn't be wise today. Instead of fighting, it's better to approach a teacher, principal, or counselor, someone who has special training in stopping bullying.

One thing is for sure: you can't ignore a bully. Bullying is a form of abuse, and it gets worse unless you deal with it. If someone is bullying you, you have to decide what you want to do. If you think you can deal with the bully yourself, start by telling the bully exactly what he or she is doing and how it makes you feel, but don't be surprised if the bully ignores your request to stop or calls you names like "sissy," "coward," or worse. I suggest you laugh if these idiotic remarks are lodged at you. This takes resilience, but you can do it. Just don't let the bully know you're offended. Bullies need to feel they can demean or hurt you. Don't play into their hands, but if the bullying doesn't stop, be prepared to get help.

This is especially important if you're being cyberbullied, which might even be more dangerous than traditional bullying. This is because the Internet allows bullies to hide and even masquerade as someone else while sending offensive and malicious messages. Cyberbullying can become vicious and can even lead to physical harassment in the offline world.

There are many forms of cyberbullying, and new forms are being invented all the time. Examples include singling out or excluding a person from an online group such as chat rooms or instant messaging; sharing personal and private information such as photos, pictures, or videos; and criticizing, fighting, or arguing in emails, chat rooms, or messaging.

You can take steps to stop a cyberbully, but under no circumstances should you engage this type of bully. Cyberbullies typically feel a great deal of hostility, anger, and pent-up aggressiveness. They want a reaction and will continue if they get one, so ignore cyberbullying, no matter what.

That said, do take the positive step of blocking the bully on as many platforms as possible and don't answer phone calls on your cell phone unless you recognize the number. You can even change your contact information if the bully keeps at you. If a bully does get through on your cell, hang up immediately and don't answer, even if you get repeated calls.

If you are being bullied, whether in person or on the Internet, you might be scared or embarrassed to tell a trusted teacher or parent, but if it continues, you are going to need help. As long as it continues, you are at risk of experiencing depression and anxiety. You might even lose sleep and experience increased feelings of sadness and loneliness. Psychologists recognize these reactions in many people who feel victimized. It isn't your fault, and you have nothing to blame yourself for. Being resilient will help you understand this and overcome the negative feelings you experience as a result of being bullied.

Confronting a traditional bully you encounter in school sometimes works, but what if the bully is your supervisor at work? After all, it isn't just kids who are bullied. Supervisors have power over you and can harass you in obvious as well as subtle ways. For example, a supervisor might give you menial work and favor other workers with the best assignments. Worse yet, a harassing supervisor can demand sexual favors without anyone around to witness what's going on. Unfortunately, some companies actually encourage favoritism and subtle forms of prejudice. Any form of prejudice is an attempt to treat others unfairly and disrespectfully.

The results of a 2014 national survey found that one-third of all workers have experienced harassment at some time in their careers[40]. For this reason, before you take a job, investigate the culture of the company. Past employees are a great source of inside information and can provide a firsthand look at how people are treated.

Industry harassment is such a serious problem that some companies have stringent policies to address offenders. While I've seen harassers terminated, I've also seen the accusing party terminated as well. If you're being harassed at work, it's best to quietly look for another job, preferably in a different company. If you make a complaint while you're still working for that company and you don't prevail, the same individual who harassed you might be the one you need a recommendation from later. You can always sue the company, as federal laws protect against workplace harassment, but I believe lawsuits are best implemented after you find another place to work. In other words, protect your interests first. This is a form of resilience.

Resilience is needed in regards to sexual orientation, too. Over 50 years ago, sex researcher Alfred Kinsey developed a scale for measuring sexual orientation ranging from "0" to describe a person who is exclusively heterosexual to "6" to describe someone who is exclusively homosexual.

---

40. "Workplace Bullying Research," *Workplace Bullying Institute*, www.workplacebullying.org/wbiresearch.

Ritch Savin Williams, a psychologist conducting interviews on sexual orientations today, estimates that only 15% of women and 5% of men fall into the mostly heterosexual category[41]. These estimates cannot be ignored.

Both sexual and gender identities are beginning to blend, particularly among young people. According to a recent survey, 20% of millennials identify as something other than strictly homosexual or cisgender, a term that describes those whose gender identity corresponds to their sex at birth.

Young LGBTQ people are clearly at variance with the general population, and I do not believe they are merely experimenting. Psychologists are already finding that these individuals experience many kinds of mistreatment, ranging from benign jokes to verbal insults to physical violence. Bullying in particular is so intense that 30% of LGBTQ children report feeling unsafe in school[42]. Many report family rejection and even being kicked out of their homes.

Once in the workplace, many LGBTQ workers report discrimination. In one experimental study, fictitious applicants were randomly assigned membership in a gay campus organization. Other applicants were not assigned membership in this organization, but otherwise, the applicants matched in every way. The result? *Gay applicants were 40% less likely to be contacted for an interview*[43].

---

41. "What Scientists Know—And Don't Know—About Sexual Orientation," *Science Daily*, April 25, 2016, https://www.sciencedaily.com/releases/2016/04/160425161342.htm.

42. Zack Ford, "Over Half of LGBT Students Feel Unsafe at School, Report Shows," *Think Progress*, October 22, 2014, https://thinkprogress.org/over-half-of-lgbt-students-feel-unsafe-at-school-report-shows-22d6fdc52b98/.

43. Hayley Fox, "Fake Job Applications Prove There's Real LGBT Discrimination in Hiring," *Take Part*, July 4, 2014, http://www.takepart.com/article/2014/07/04/fake-resumes-show-real-anti-lgbt-discrimination.

Barry M. Cohen, PhD

As young people come out more and more, society will perhaps become more tolerant, but that remains to be seen. However, on college campuses today, young people of all kinds of sexual and gender preferences are becoming more common. Among their peers, I believe they will increasingly find acceptance, and the implications for society are huge. The need for accommodation starts in families and extends to workplaces and schools. The need for resilience—on everyone's part—is just as evident.

Bullying and harassment cause great stress, but you will experience just as many or even more problems caused by conflicts with people in everyday life. All children get into disagreements and arguments. Some of them look silly in hindsight, but we always remember how they made us feel. Conflicts can be so hurtful that they lead to violence and worse. Every day, needless deaths are caused by conflicts that lead to rage.

Conflicts that are easy to resolve don't take a lot of teamwork, resourcefulness, or resilience, but other conflicts are more complicated. Say your dad wants to finish a report he urgently needs for work, but your mom wants his help clearing out some closets to prepare for out-of-town visitors. If you're resilient, I suspect you can figure out some solutions. After all, this is an easy conflict to resolve.

A moderately difficult conflict to resolve might involve a spouse who is jealous of the close relationships her husband is developing with her extended family. She demands more time, feels neglected and hurt, and accuses certain family members of ruining her marriage. What to do? It will take resilience to figure out how to handle this sensitive situation. It can be done, but it must be done carefully.

A very difficult conflict that nearly shut down a company involved an aggressive union with a reputation for not bargaining in good faith that won a hard-fought election to represent the employees. Management had formerly had the authority to make compensation and benefits decisions, but now the executives were being forced to deal with a union they didn't know well or trust. On the day before contract negotiations were due to start, the union called a surprise strike. Most employees stayed home, but a few tried to cross the picket line. Fights developed, and a manager was badly hurt and hospitalized. Successfully resolving this conflict required both management and employees to exhibit a tremendous amount of teamwork, resourcefulness, and resilience.

Regretfully, few individuals are taught how to resolve conflicts in school. Whatever your age, you're likely going to have to learn mostly by trial and error, and this will require resilience. Keep in mind that if you learn the wisdoms I've shared about maturity and resourcefulness, you will at least have a head start. Here are some other constructive suggestions for how to handle conflicts with resilience:

- Seek "win-win" solutions that reasonably satisfy both parties.

- Avoid "lose-lose" solutions that more or less frustrate both parties; in such situations, conflict is likely to continue even if a truce is temporarily called.

- Recognize that "win-lose" solutions can make matters worse in the long run; one party walks away reasonably satisfied and the other doesn't, which means bad feelings remain and the conflict often worsens.

Personal awareness training can help teach conflict resolution skills. Those who find themselves in tough negotiations could benefit from the insights of psychologist Maya Tamar[44]. Intuitively, she notes, people become angry, especially if the negotiations turn to "win-lose." Still, she contends that anger can be an "approach emotion." If you can stay in control and present your anger in a measured and articulate manner, you can argue more effectively. However, if your anger leads to yelling, accusing, blaming, swearing, or putting your opponent down, it can make things worse. What is needed, says Dr. Tamar, is assertive use of anger, which can move both parties to seek new or different viable solutions.

---

44. Shirli Kopelman, "Make Your Emotions Work for You in Negotiations," *Harvard Business Review*, May 16, 2014, https://hbr.org/2014/05/make-your-emotions-work-for-you-in-negotiations.

The following tips offer a crash course on how to use resilience to successfully reach win-win solutions.

How to Use Resilience to Reach Win-Win Solutions

1. Objectively define the problem and determine what the conflict is. Refrain from accusing or blaming other parties and stick to the topic at hand. Not until both parties can agree on what they're facing can solutions be realistically addressed.

2. Stay in the present. If you bring up troubling history, the dialogue will quickly deteriorate.

3. Use "I" language, not "you" language, to describe the problem. "You" language puts conflicting parties on the defensive, especially if they distrust one another. For example, note the difference in the following two sentences. Which would you rather be on the receiving end of?

You always scream and yell at me when we disagree with one another. You don't respect me. Why don't you grow up!

or

I hate it when you raise your voice and scream at me when we disagree with one another. It makes me feel that you don't respect me.

4. Offer ideas for how you would like to see the problem resolved. Present only one idea at a time and keep the solution focused on the present and future. The past isn't something anyone can change.

5. Allow the other party to consider your solution. Don't expect instant agreement. New solutions have to fit well before they can be accepted.

6. Allow the other party to present an idea for you to consider. Weigh this idea carefully. This will build respect and prime the pump for finding common ground.

If you can keep the focus on how the different parties can reach a common agreement, you're more than halfway home, but if no solutions seem viable, take a break and allow both parties to be resourceful and come up with fresh solutions.

Perhaps the toughest aspect of solving problems involves learning how to communicate successfully. This, too, takes resilience, because it's easier to miscommunicate than it is to communicate clearly. Why is this the case? Most of us can talk well enough, so why do we still struggle to communicate without being misinterpreted?

Psychologists know that people are as distinct as snowflakes. The range of individual differences is huge. Some people are painful introverts while others are flaming extroverts. Some are so optimistic they can't see things for what they are. Others are so pessimistic that their every thought turns other people off. Personalities vary a great deal, and some people are just plain complicated.

It takes great patience—an aspect of resilience—to communicate with difficult people. Overly aggressive and conniving people will certainly test your patience, but painfully shy people can be just as challenging. As much as possible, draw people to you who will inspire you to perform your best. If you're lucky enough to have a great mentor or two in your life, cherish these people and learn all you can from them.

My earliest memorable experience with conflict resolution occurred when I was 30 years old. I was buying something at a local convenience store when the owner spoke rudely to me. He claimed I was wasting his time as I shopped, and he demanded that I buy something or get out of his store. I became very angry and walked out of the store in a huff. Afterward, I became upset at myself for letting him treat me with disrespect. I also realized I was frightened at being confronted in this way.

A short time later, I attended a personal awareness program that included a segment on managing conflict. I shared the confrontation I'd had with the store owner and then practiced confronting him using role playing. I was amazed at what I learned about myself. Conflict panicked me! It brought back fearful times with the bully in my childhood. I needed to be resilient to deal with this.

Gradually, I learned how to assert myself without being aggressive. Assertiveness is a must for communicating well in conflicts and is equally critical for successfully dealing with confrontations and aggressive people.

Fortunately, it can be learned. Assertiveness became a lifelong skill and part of my ever-growing maturity and ability to be resilient.

In sum, here are my life wisdoms about resiliency:

- Resilient people bounce back from life's trying times and crises. They feel stress, but when they're under the gun, they don't withdraw or give up. They can tough things out.

- People need resilience in the face of ongoing trying events that last for many years or even a lifetime. Caregiving causes long-term stress and requires resilience.

- No one is born resilient; it is learned largely from experience.

- Strong family ties and good friends help a lot when you face tough times; you can draw emotional strength from them and also from your faith.

- Do not underestimate the power of teams when facing a crisis; teams can be a great source of inspiration and superior problem solving.

- Most people underestimate their ability to lead others, especially in a crisis; great leaders often emerge when they're needed most.

- The worst disagreeable people are abusers who dominate and hurt others physically and emotionally. Abusers are motivated by self-hatred turned outward against their defenseless victims. If you're in an abusive relationship, get out as soon as you can. Abusers rarely change.

- Bullies are close cousins of abusers. They pick on and humiliate others and delight in taunting people weaker than themselves. Bullies are very common in companies, too. They harass other workers, and sometimes they bully less powerful employees to get sexual or other favors.

- Cyberbullying comes in many forms on the Internet, and more forms are being invented all the time. Cyberbullies are emotionally troubled people. To avoid being a victim of these individuals, do not respond to their hateful games, no matter what. Ignore them completely and block them from as many social media platforms as possible. In addition, if you are being cyberbullied, do not answer your cell phone unless you recognize the number.

- Conflicts are common. Almost no one learns how to resolve conflict in school or even on the job. Resolving conflict successfully takes resilience plus a mutually agreed-on and objective description of the problem. Without agreement, most attempts at resolving conflicts are fruitless or make matters worse.

- Successful careers require communication with all kinds of people, including difficult ones. The art of communicating requires far more than eloquent talking.

- If you're lucky, you will have one or two great mentors in your life. Draw on their wisdom when dealing with hurtful and disagreeable individuals. Great mentors are models of maturity, resourcefulness, and resilience.

Recommended Readings

Internet References

"Bullying," *Wikipedia,* last modified March 18, 2018. https://en.wikipedia.org/wiki/Bullying, accessed April 9, 2018.

"Bullying Statistics." *Pacer's National Bullying Prevention Center*, 2018. http://www.pacer.org/bullying/resources/stats.asp.

End to Cyber Bullying Organization. www.endcyberbullying.org.

Ford, Zack. "Over Half of LGBT Students Feel Unsafe at School, Report Shows." *Think Progress*, October 22, 2014. https://thinkprogress.

org/over-half-of-lgbt-students-feel-unsafe-at-school-report-shows-22d6fdc52b98/.

Fox, Hayley. "Fake Job Applications Prove There's Real LGBT Discrimination in Hiring." *Take Part*, July 4, 2014. http://www.takepart.com/article/2014/07/04/fake-resumes-show-real-anti-lgbt-discrimination.

Harrar, Sari. "14 Ways to Resolve Conflicts and Solve Relationship Problems." *Reader's Digest*, 2018. https://www.rd.com/advice/relationships/14-ways-resolve-conflicts-and-solve-relationship-problems/.

Help Guide, 2018. www.helpguide.org.

"How Is Bullying Defined?" *Pacer's National Bullying Prevention Center*, 2018. http://www.pacer.org/bullying/resources/questions-answered/how-is-bullying-defined.asp.

"How to Manage Conflict." *WikiHow*, 2018. https://www.wikihow.com/Manage-Conflict.

Kopelman, Shirli. "Make Your Emotions Work for You in Negotiations." *Harvard Business Review*, May 16, 2014. https://hbr.org/2014/05/make-your-emotions-work-for-you-in-negotiations.

Mills, Harry, and Dombeck, Mark. "Resilience: Optimism." *Gracepoint*, 2017. https://www.gracepointwellness.org/298-emotional-resilience/article/5789-resilience-optimism.

"Resilience: Build Skills to Endure Hardship." *Mayo Clinic*, 2018. https://www.mayoclinic.org/tests-procedures/resilience-training/in-depth/resilience/art-20046311.

"Search Results for: Articles Domestic." *Help Guide*, 2018. https://helpguide.org/search/mysearch.php?zoom_sort=0&zoom_query=articles+domestic&zoom_per_page=20&zoom_and=1.

"Stop Cyberbullying." *Fund for Civility, Respect, and Understanding.* http://fundforcivility.org/stop-cyberbullying/.

"The Road to Resilience." *American Psychological Association*, 2018. http://www.apa.org/helpcenter/road-resilience.aspx.

"Tips for Managing Conflict." *Clarke University*, 2018. https://www.clarke.edu/campus-life/health-wellness/counseling/articles-advice/tips-for-managing-conflict/.

"What Scientists Know—And Don't Know—About Sexual Orientation." *Science Daily*, April 25, 2016. https://www.sciencedaily.com/releases/2016/04/160425161342.htm.

"Workplace Bullying Research." *Workplace Bullying Institute.* www.workplacebullying.org/wbiresearch.

Print References

Large, R., & R. K. White. "Experimental Study of Leadership and Group Life." *Readings in Social Psychology*, 1958.

Steinmetz, Katy. "A New Identity: Beyond He or She." *Time*, 2017, 189, 11, 48–54.

Chapter 13:

Career Success

WHEN YOUR CAREER IS OVER, you might want to look back over it, but save the regrets. Everyone who has retired has plenty of "should have" and "could have" stories to tell, but as Shakespeare so aptly put it, "What is done cannot be undone." In other words, a past career is history.

Until you reach this point, it's important to take deliberate steps to search for a career that fits your unique personality and interests. When I started teaching university students, I was shocked to realize that most had only a vague understanding of their natural talents and almost none understood their own motivations and interests.

Because it's bewildering to ponder the many possible fields of work, my advice is to take stock of yourself. First, ask yourself what you have no interest in doing. In other words, start by eliminating entire fields of work that you find unsuitable. If you're not an animal lover, working with animals is out. If you don't like math, engineering and statistical jobs will drive you crazy. After finishing your elimination list, identify the things you do enjoy and (hopefully) do well.

I call this list your first pass at your assets. If you created a part-time service business as a kid and liked it, entrepreneurial jobs might be for you. If you enjoy leadership experiences, management or public service jobs might interest you. If you like taking care of people or volunteering in a hospital or clinic, health care jobs might be right for you. If you work with your hands and have a knack for fixing things, trade jobs might be a great fit.

If you struggle to spell out your unique assets, ask your parents and best friends what they think you do well and might enjoy. Everyone has "manifest interests," and people who know you well will likely recognize them. If you need help, ask your school counselor to give you an interest inventory of many different activities to help you identify what most appeals to you. You can also take career inventories online and join professional organizations that allow you to talk with peers and even business leaders.

Starting in high school, you can join organizations that help you develop confidence, leadership skills, character, and more while honing your skills. Then, as you transition to university life, you will have already begun walking the path to personal growth. Business-related organizations flourish at universities and are often connected to the business world. By getting involved, you increase your potential career opportunities.

Now is the time to introduce you to three very important words: networking, networking, networking. Okay, so it's one word three times. So many jobs or opportunities are found through networking that it pays to repeat this word! Business organizations from real estate to security to accounting allow college students and others to join or at least attend meetings where they can meet and interact with people in the working world who have jobs they might be interested in.

If you still have no idea what kind of career you might want, visit your school's website to see what majors or vocational courses you could study. Prioritize the top ones that interest you and talk to an instructor in that department about possible jobs. The Bureau of Labor Statistics publishes the *Occupational Outlook Handbook* that gives all the information you need to learn about these jobs and many more. Get up-to-date information about the job markets for those careers you think might be a good fit. You can narrow your options further by studying employment prospects in various locations where you might want to study and eventually live.

When I began college, I had no idea what to study. Neither of my parents went to college, and they were of little help. I was wearing braces on my teeth, and my dentist thought I might like dentistry. With nothing more than that to go on, I naively chose pre-medicine as my college major. I found these classes tedious and boring, but I did well in them.

Grade success might tell you that you can master a subject, but career success involves much more than that. I would have been a horrible dentist, and eventually I figured that out. I have no mechanical ability and my spatial perception is poor. What was I thinking?

A career is a series of related jobs in a given field. Career success is defined by how productive and satisfied you are at your chosen career. Good grades in related classes are far from the best criteria to use when assessing how suitable a career might be. If you don't find your current studies interesting, look further. Try different areas of study. Talk to people in careers you do find intriguing. The old adage "Seek and you shall find" is good advice when seeking a career you will enjoy. At the very least, you might discover some new interests or talents. Remember, understanding yourself is the basis of all wisdom.

After giving up dentistry as a potential career, I took an introductory course in psychology. I found it interesting, but I got a lower grade than I'd earned in my pre-med courses! I had underestimated my competition. Grades were determined on a "curve," and my competition was stiff.

I decided to take another psychology course. This time I tried applied psychology. My first course was in industrial psychology, and the professor had an active consulting practice in addition to his teaching career. I loved the course and earned one of the highest grades in class, so I decided to visit the library to read about different careers in psychology. I learned that industrial psychologists were at the top of the pay range. These careers paid much more than psychologists earned in health settings or schools, but those jobs attracted me too because they involved counseling and therapy.

I began taking every applied psychology course I could find. I took courses in related fields, too, such as psychological testing and counseling. By the time I began graduate school, I had much more training than most of my fellow graduate students. In hindsight, my grades in graduate school were excellent partly due to my superb undergraduate training.

Then two bombs dropped right on my head. The war in Vietnam was raging. I almost was drafted, but I managed to get a last-minute student deferment. Columbia University dropped the second bomb when it suddenly discontinued its doctoral program. I could have earned my doctorate in a related field at Columbia, but most of those psychologists worked in education, an area I wasn't interested in. Getting accepted into a doctoral industrial psychology program with a master's degree wasn't easy! Most of those programs selected their grad students straight out of college, but when a new program in industrial psychology accepted me, I left my family and fiancé to finish my studies far from home.

In hindsight, this was one of the best experiences I ever had. My professors came from all over the country, and many had several years of industrial experiences and active consulting practices. I learned state-of-the-art skills from some of the leading industrial psychologists in the country. I even did a doctoral internship at JCPenney's corporate headquarters, where several global corporations were also headquartered, and had lunch with Mr. Penney!

Speaking of finishing studies far from home, studying abroad for a semester or more while in college can be very helpful. College students can really grow when they immerse themselves in a new culture, make new friends, troubleshoot new challenges, and accept unfamiliar opportunities, all the while gaining skills that will be useful for their resumes and careers. The fact is, taking the opportunity to study abroad and gain these valuable experiences is much easier for college kids than for those who have entered the working world and are paying rent and holding down a job.

Career success takes a lot of hard work, preparation, and talent, but serendipity also helps. If Columbia University hadn't terminated its program, I never would have gotten the fine training I received. It was just dumb luck that I found an exceptional program. The draft board was at my heels, and I needed to enroll somewhere fast! I learned that to succeed in a career, you must decide to do it and not let yourself be sidetracked, no matter what.

When you start a career, it's very unlikely you'll know where it will take you. Most individuals change jobs at least a handful of times. Some people get disillusioned or face setbacks in their careers. The average executive experiences at least two job derailments or setbacks, and getting promoted is no sure thing[45]. The average small business has about a 50-50 chance of survival after five years[46]. In case it's not yet clear, resilience will be your greatest asset when it comes to managing your career.

Along the way, you'll likely receive many tempting job offers. Recruiters might try to attract you elsewhere, but before you leave a job or take your first offer, step back and evaluate the situation carefully. There's always an "opportunity cost" involved in turning down a job offer. If you're not careful, the one you pass up might be better than the one you take. Think cautiously and carefully and beware of personal blind spots.

Also look into the long-term job security of the company you're considering. Is security important to you, especially if you're young and likely to change jobs anyway? Is the culture of the company a good fit? Do you want to use this job as a steppingstone for networking in your industry? What about benefits, especially specialized training that helps you acquire career-enhancing skills and expertise? The website Glassdoor.com has salary estimates for jobs and companies based on current and former employees who also often leave reviews of company culture and conditions.

There are so many factors to consider besides starting compensation. Don't be blinded by the offer of a great salary! Remember, the younger you are, the more risks you can take. Your starting salary is less important than how much money you can command as your career develops and what attractive offers might be presented to you if you have a strong resume and advanced training from a state-of-the-art company.

Along those lines, millennials entering the workforce should be careful to mindfully emphasize any and all relevant experience. This includes college internships and part-time jobs as well as applicable student activities.

---

45. Carl Robinson, "Preventing Executive Derailment," *Leadership Consulting*, 2009, http://leadershipconsulting.com/preventing-executive-derailment/.

46. "Startup Business Failure Rate by Industry," *Statistic Brain*, 2018, https://www.statisticbrain.com/startup-failure-by-industry/.

Changing careers is also becoming more common. Some individuals literally drop out of traditional jobs mid career to begin non-traditional ones. A dentist might abruptly sell her practice and become a missionary in a foreign country. A teacher might retire early and start his own cupcake bakery. A university professor might decide to leave her post even though she has tenure in order to start her own consulting practice.

That was me. I had three jobs in my career. I was a university professor, then a consulting psychologist, and finally a business owner and head of my own consulting firm managing other industrial psychologists.

If you're looking for a job, utilize social media. Most companies have websites that provide a great deal of information. Many individuals also develop a presence on Facebook and LinkedIn. Often, you can learn about the style of a company (Formal? Hierarchical? Informal? Team focused?) by viewing its Facebook page. Also remember that these same companies might look at your Facebook page during the interview process. Hence, only post what society considers to be acceptable and non-abrasive.

LinkedIn can introduce you to many people and can help you find opportunities. As you build connections (set a goal of at least 500), you will no doubt find that someone you're connected to has a connection to a company you're interested in. You might then have them "introduce" you to someone at this company.

LinkedIn is free, but you can pay for additional features to enhance your job search. Review other people's profiles and see what makes them stand out, then edit your profile until it looks and feels professional. Every time you earn a degree or specialized certification, add it to your profile. Making a change flags hiring managers and headhunters and often leads to interviews. Writing or even re-posting an article can also help differentiate you. If you blind apply in order to find a job, reach out to someone you know linked to the company to let them know you've applied. If you send an email, include the job title and a few lines about how your skill set fits their need. Once you create your profile, get your friends and college buddies to do it as well, then link to each other.

If you're having trouble finding email addresses or even phone numbers and physical addresses, try joining www.connect.data.com, which lists tens of thousands of contacts at many companies. You can either buy credits or provide information on people you know to gain credits that you can use to view full information. This enables you to email or call senior managers, which in turn might yield job leads. Think out of the box, and roadblocks become challenges.

Here are some additional tips for mindfully managing your career:

- Network purposively rather than aimlessly and maintain long-lasting industry relationships. Also keep your close colleagues in other organizations abreast of what you're doing. When trusted co-workers go to work for other companies, stay in touch. You never know when they might hear of a great opportunity that's suitable for you.

- Attend industry conferences and take leadership roles in major industry associations. Meet influential people who can impact your career and stay as visible as possible. Explore but don't jump when new opportunities come your way. Do your homework about the culture of any possible new opportunities. Past employees can be a great source of inside information.

- Beware of tiny missteps that can derail your career. This includes dressing sloppily, showing excessive cleavage, talking in an unpolished way, making tactless or childish remarks, or telling off-color jokes.

- Perfect your interviewing skills and practice them as often as you can. A good way to learn interviewing skills is to interview other people. Being on the other side of the desk will give you new insight into what good interviewers look for and how they probe for evidence of demonstrated talents.

- To succeed in your current job, be prepared to accept lateral moves. Some organizations like to develop people who can "switch hit." Small organizations in particular value versatility among employees.

Your talents will propel your career forward if you wisely manage your strengths. Keep in mind that overusing a single strength can become a weakness that limits you[47]. For example, perhaps you're a great listener and demonstrate it frequently. Perhaps you only talk when you're absolutely sure you've heard everyone out. Then again, when you do speak, perhaps you're terse and don't mince your words. If this describes you, you might be coming across as passive *or* aggressive to the point that others don't look to you for leadership.

Learn to use your strengths in concert with each another. Great listeners who understand exactly what others are saying can become genuinely great communicators. Likewise, if you can show understanding and empathy when people talk, they will begin listening to what you have to say. Throw in a few intriguing open-ended questions, and you can start to facilitate dialogue and even initiate attempts to lead others. The art of communicating encompasses far more than great listening, though this is a powerful skill.

Other overdone strengths can backfire, too. If you're highly tenacious, you can come across as a bulldog or, worse yet, as stubborn and even inflexible. At the other extreme, if you're highly flexible, you can come across as unsure of yourself and indecisive.

Even highly intelligent people sometimes overdo their strengths. I once consulted with a smart, resourceful executive who freely offered his solutions at senior management meetings. Although his ideas were excellent, other senior people began to tire of him. He came across as an egotist and know-it-all because he literally drowned out his peers. He had all the smarts he needed to succeed, but he lacked the sensitivity and maturity to recognize the power of teamwork. With my coaching, he learned how to be a team player and a follower. The senior team continued to use his ingenuity, and once he no longer gave long lectures, he became valued for his ideas and innovative solutions.

---

47. Susan Biali, "Don't Let Your Strengths Become Your Weakness," *Psychology Today,* May 10, 2013, https://www.psychologytoday.com/us/blog/prescriptions-life/201305/don-t-let-your-strengths-become-your-weakness.

Learn the art of managing your strengths. Use all your talents, mixing them up to maximize your effectiveness. If your talents are the orchestra and you are the conductor, your job is to create great music using all your talents in sync with one another.

A caution: be careful not to over-rely on technology to do your work. There's good evidence that pilots who over-rely on computer instruments to fly their planes don't get enough flying time to sharpen their piloting skills[48]. Likewise, surgeons who use computer-assisted technologies to perform robotic surgeries run the risk of underutilizing their skills[49]. Architects using computer-assisted design (CAD) programs face the same risk[50]. Technology can make us more productive and efficient, but don't over-rely on it. To stay current and improve, your skills must be utilized. What's more, they need to be the right skills that hiring managers are searching for.

For example, a 2015 study determined that hiring managers held a number of beliefs about the perceived strengths and weaknesses of potential millennial candidates[51]. Specifically, hiring managers were seeking:

---

48. Andy Pasztor, "Pilots Rely Too Much on Automation, Panel Says," *Wall Street Journal,* November 17, 2013, https://www.wsj.com/articles/pilots-rely-too-much-on-automation-panel-says-1384749188.

49. Jennifer Polland, "Watch: This Robot Is Poised to Change Surgery Forever," *Business Insider,* August 1, 2012, www.businessinsider.com/the-future-of-robotic-surgery-2012-7.

50. Roger K. Lewis, "Computers Are Great Tools for Architects, But Don't Let CAD Go Wild," *Washington Post,* February 11, 2011, http://www.washingtonpost.com/wp-dyn/content/article/2011/02/11/AR2011021103539.html.

51. Miriam Salpeter, "5 Secrets to Career Success in 2015," *U.S. News,* November 4, 2014, https://money.usnews.com/money/blogs/outside-voices-careers/2014/11/04/5-secrets-to-career-success-in-2015.

- *Strong technical and hard skills.* Personality was nice, too, but hiring managers favored candidates with strong technical and hard skills over personality, something they believed millennials were trained in.

- *Innovation and resourcefulness.* As of 2015, hiring managers believed millennials were more open to change (72%), creative (66%), and adaptive (66%) than their Gen X counterparts.

- *Team players.* Alas, hiring managers believed millennials weren't as strong on teamwork (27%) as Gen X workers. Millennials who wish to counter this belief should work to develop team skills early and show evidence that they can be a good fit for the organization.

- *Company loyalty.* Hiring managers value loyalty, yet 58% of millennials reported that they expected to stay in their jobs fewer than three years. It might be advisable for millennials to communicate their willingness to stay longer if their company is willing to develop them and give them career-enhancing skills.

- *Career flexibility.* Hiring managers were more interested in potential employees who were willing and able to pursue different types of jobs, whether they were millennials or not.

While some stereotypes about millennials in the workforce are less than complimentary, small business consultant Emily Richett contends that millennials can be great assets[52]. They are eager to learn and open to feedback, but given their youth and reliance on the Internet and modern technology, they also present unique challenges. She recommends that businesses develop an employee handbook for millennials covering such topics as the use of social media, dress code, and other behaviors.

---

52. Emily Richett, "5 Situations You Need to Address with New Hires before Things Get Awkward," *Inc.*, March 8, 2017, https://www.inc.com/emily-richett/5-situations-you-need-to-address-with-every-new-hire-ranked-by-awkwardness.html.

Potentially awkward work situations Richett addresses include the following:

- Client conversations. Millennials are supremely comfortable using text messages and social media, but conversational skills are important, too. The handbook might spell out the company's expectations for what is appropriate and not appropriate regarding conversations with clients. For example, a new hire should keep current on topics of interest to clients that are presented in trade journals and popular business articles and be able and willing to discuss these topics.

- Casual dress code. Millennials enjoy casual dress, but the handbook should spell out what's appropriate, including whether or not items such as leggings, sneakers, and lightly washed denim jeans are appropriate for the workplace.

- Email etiquette. Both the tone and preferred style of emails should be spelled out in the handbook with examples of appropriate written communications. Even a short probationary period of reviewing emails might be advisable for new hires.

Here are some surprising 2017 survey results about millennials in the workplace: just 18% of millennials find the workplace a fun place to work, and a whopping 55% report being disengaged from their work[53]. This is a disturbing finding, since millennials are now the largest generation in the workplace. It suggests that businesses have a lot to learn about millennials, and vice versa!

Since millennials desire a personal connection to causes, companies should link their mission statements to causes millennials support. Millennials have a strong sense of responsibility, but large external charities do not move them as deeply as local charities. In addition, millennials strongly

---

53. "Attract Emerging Leaders with Purpose, Not Perks," *University of Notre Dame*, 2018, https://ethicalleadership.nd.edu/news/attract-emerging-leaders-with-purpose-not-perks/.

favor supervisors who focus on their personal development, so supervisors who must give negative feedback should be very careful to connect it to skill development that will enhance millennials' long-term success. Millennials see flexibility as a signal of trust, so flexible working conditions are a plus. Finally, creating fun perks such as on-site acupuncture, free travel, and nap pods creates a positive work environment that could help attract talented millennials.

I worked with one global company that gave all its employees worldwide the perk of paying for one course each year. *Any* course was acceptable, including courses that delved into personal interests and hobbies!

There is no magic formula for career success, but it's wise to ponder recent advice from an article in the *Wall Street Journal*[54]: find out as early as you can how your supervisor plans to evaluate your job performance. This information will help you know what work is valued and put you on a course to succeed. In addition, as you build a relationship with your boss, take every opportunity to ask specific questions about how you're doing. Just be sure to listen closely without bristling or getting defensive if you hear something upsetting. Stay calm and professional and solicit advice on how you can improve. Remember, your boss is the ideal person to coach you to succeed, so welcome assignments that stretch you. In fact, ask your boss to think of you when such assignments are being planned.

Your boss is not the only person who can help you succeed. Ask for criticism from colleagues who will tell you the truth. Compare your performance to co-workers who excel at their jobs. This will motivate you to set stretch goals for yourself and help you further engage with the work at hand.

Finally, it is up to you to establish and maintain collaborative relationships with the people around you. That includes everyone from supervisors to

---

54. Sue Shellenbarger, "How to Know When You're on Thin Ice at Work," *Wall Street Journal*, October 24, 2017, https://www.wsj.com/articles/how-to-know-when-youre-on-thin-ice-at-work-1508857912.

subordinates and definitely your peers. Never let yourself become isolated, naively thinking that if you excel at the technical side of your job, you will be valued and eventually promoted. That simply is seldom, if ever, the case. Surround yourself with others you enjoy, but never forget to seek out high performers and support staff who can help you succeed. In other words, a large part of career success depends on how collaborative you are. Those with strong team skills have the competitive advantage when it comes to getting the best assignments as well as valuable coaching from others.

Career success isn't a given, but it's certainly rewarding when it happens. In sum, here are my wisdoms for career success:

- A career is a life journey. It consists of a series of related jobs within a chosen field of work. Most high school and college students are bewildered by the many choices they have and don't know how to narrow their search for a career that suits their interests and talents.

- There's more than one career for everyone. To find a career that interests you, take stock of your talents, interests, and skills. Remember, wisdom requires you to understand yourself. Many people can help you in your search for a suitable career, and you can even take online inventories to learn more about yourself. I hope that every individual who reads this book finds a demanding and rewarding career!

- Career success takes a lot of talent, preparation, and hard work, but don't discount luck or what I call "serendipity." Take every opportunity that comes your way. Don't get sidetracked. Keep moving forward in the face of obstacles. Tenacity counts!

- Some people experience career derailment. It happens more often than you might think. If you want to start your own business, you have a 50-50 chance of making a go of it over the first five years.

- People make career changes all the time. If your work is comfortable but doesn't energize you, find something else to do. It's your life, and it's up to you to live it to the fullest.

- Network actively throughout your career. You will find more opportunities by word of mouth than you ever glean from a recruiter or employment ads.

- Be especially careful not to rely on a single talent. An overused strength can become a weakness. Consider yourself an orchestra leader responsible for utilizing your many talents. Use them all so you can give dependably great performances!

Recommended Readings

Internet References

"Attract Emerging Leaders with Purpose, Not Perks." *University of Notre Dame*, 2018. https://ethicalleadership.nd.edu/news/attract-emerging-leaders-with-purpose-not-perks/.

Biali, Susan. "Don't Let Your Strengths become Your Weakness." *Psychology Today,* May 10, 2013. https://www.psychologytoday.com/us/blog/prescriptions-life/201305/don-t-let-your-strengths-become-your-weakness.

Bureau of Labor Statistics. www.bls.gov/ooh.

Chernoff, Marc. "40 Quick Tips for Career Happiness and Success." *Marc & Angel Hack Life,* February 26, 2008. http://www.marcandangel.com/2008/02/26/40-quick-tips-for-career-happiness-and-success/.

Pasztor, Andy. "Pilots Rely Too Much on Automation, Panel Says." *The Wall Street Journal,* November 17, 2013. https://www.wsj.com/articles/pilots-rely-too-much-on-automation-panel-says-1384749188.

Polland, Jennifer. "Watch: This Robot Is Poised to Change Surgery Forever." *Business Insider*, August 1, 2012. www.businessinsider.com/the-future-of-robotic-surgery-2012-7.

Richett, Emily. "5 Situations You Need to Address with New Hires before Things Get Awkward." *Inc.*, March 8, 2017. https://www.inc.com/emily-richett/5-situations-you-need-to-address-with-every-new-hire-ranked-by-awkwardness.html.

Robinson, Carl. "Preventing Executive Derailment." *Leadership Consulting*, 2009. http://leadershipconsulting.com/preventing-executive-derailment/.

Salpeter, Miriam. "5 Secrets to Career Success in 2015." *U.S. News*, November 4, 2014. https://money.usnews.com/money/blogs/outside-voices-careers/2014/11/04/5-secrets-to-career-success-in-2015.

Shellenbarger, Sue. "How to Know When You're on Thin Ice at Work." *Wall Street Journal*, October 24, 2017. https://www.wsj.com/articles/how-to-know-when-youre-on-thin-ice-at-work-1508857912.

"Startup Business Failure Rate by Industry." *Statistic Brain*, 2018. https://www.statisticbrain.com/startup-failure-by-industry/.

Chapter 14:

Savvy Financial Habits

Some lucky individuals inherit great wealth or win the lottery, but most of us aren't so fortunate. My parents never acquired wealth, but I did. To do this, I first had to learn sound wealth habits by observing others. Mostly, I learned what not to do by observing those who got into financial difficulties or invested poorly.

As a child, I received a small weekly allowance. After graduating from high school, I attended a city college that was free to students with exceptional grades. As mentioned earlier, I was delighted to live at home and commute to college. If I needed money for a big date or weekend holiday, I got part-time work counting inventory at department stores, something computers do today.

My student days taught me a lot about good financial habits. For starters, you must have self-discipline to acquire wealth. If you spend more than you bring in, you will quickly get into a financial hole. Some people never get out of debt because they keep buying things they can't afford. It all starts with your buying habits, savings habits, and smart investing.

Second, never take your eyes off your end goal. I paid cash for everything I purchased in college. If I didn't have the cash, I went without and learned to save for what I wanted. Today, students are bombarded with credit card offers, many with outlandish monthly interest rates of up to 18% or more. Anyone who can't pay their bill in full within one month is charged a late fee and interest that accumulates each succeeding month until it's paid.

A recent survey of the American Institutes of Certified Public Accountants revealed that over 25% of millennials had late credit card payments or were dealing with bill collectors[55]. Surprisingly, seven out of 10 millennials believed they were "financially stable" if they were able to pay their bills every month. In nearly every case, that's not so!

Credit cards are an invitation to get into debt early in life, but if you use them wisely, they can help you build your credit score, something you will need in the likely event that you will someday want to take out a mortgage or borrow money to purchase a car. Individuals are routinely turned down for loans for these large necessities because of low credit scores. This sober fact should be reason enough to encourage millennials to buy wisely and save diligently!

Debt was a challenge when I began graduate school at Columbia University. I went from paying nothing as an undergraduate to paying $60 a credit for my master's degree work. Today, that tuition costs almost $1,500 a credit. Ironically, my undergraduate courses were often as good if not better than my first-year graduate courses!

When I started at Columbia, I began working part-time as a personnel interviewer at a local manufacturing company, but I still needed a federal student loan to help pay for my studies. I was lucky, as the loan didn't have to be paid back for 10 years after I received my degree. Even better, the loan

---

55. "Better Money Habits Millennial Report," *Bank of America*, 2018, https://bettermoneyhabits.bankofamerica.com/en/millennial-report.

would be forgiven if I taught after I graduated. That said, if I didn't finish, I had to pay back the loan immediately. I began to think about becoming a university professor because of that loan!

If you must take out a loan, search far and wide for the best interest terms. Do not just accept the first loan you're offered. Borrow as little as possible. Get a part-time job to help pay some of your tuition. Some universities offer assistantships for work you do on campus and will waive all or part of your tuition. In my case, working in my field was a great way to build my experiences and portfolio while limiting my debt.

To get a Ph.D., I knew at least four years of graduate study lay ahead. Success would require discipline, more excellent grades, and sacrifice (part-time work while studying). Here's the wealth lesson: make certain you're passionate about the career you choose, then commit to accomplishing your goal. Build your portfolio as early as possible. Internships and related part-time jobs look great on your resume once you begin searching for your first real job.

Here's another wealth lesson: get inventive when you're poor. It wasn't important that I earn a lot during my long years of graduate study; it was important that I learn a lot. Graduate students manage to scrimp by on very little. I remember buying an unfinished door, buying legs for it, and using it for my desk. With that plus a cheap fluorescent desk lamp, I was all set. I could spread out my books and papers on an invented desk that was bigger than any fancy desk I'd ever seen. Years later, it was fun to laugh at how frugal I was.

After finishing my master's degree, I started a doctoral program at the University of Tennessee. Tuition was much less expensive than at Columbia, and I managed to enroll as an in-state student. The last thing I wanted was another student loan. Eventually, I got a fellowship that covered all my expenses, including my tuition. Things began looking up financially. Good study habits, self-discipline, living within my meager means, and keeping my focus on my studies all contributed to my sound wealth habits.

I ended up finishing my eight years of university work with almost no debt, and because I began teaching as a college professor, my federal loan was entirely waived. Clearly, my financial habits were set early. Set yours early, too. Otherwise, the noose of debt can choke you, and some people never manage to loosen it.

Remember Benjamin Franklin's expression? A penny saved *is* a penny earned. I took that sentiment to heart and began saving as soon as I began working. Later, when I was earning a lot of money from my consulting practice, I saved even more. I even socked away a lot of money in a company pension plan. It grew rapidly, and the tax on that money wasn't due until I began withdrawing the money during my retirement years. Wealth lesson: even if you're earning a lot of money, live beneath your means and make saving a regular part of your life. You will never regret it!

America's wealthy offer all of us great lessons for acquiring money over a lifetime[56]. These money lessons might surprise you:

- They earn a lot of money largely from owning their own businesses. A full 86% of them put in more than 50 hours a week.

- The wealthy start saving as soon as they can. Almost 40% of their income goes into savings!

- Most wealthy Americans do not rent; they own their own homes to build equity, get tax breaks, and make a profit when they sell.

- The wealthiest Americans go on six vacations a year, but they are not extravagant. 77% of them fly economy class.

No doubt this is why a recent Bank of America survey of thousands of millennials and millennial parents left the bankers scratching their heads[57].

---

56. Kevin Voigt, "8 Habits of Self-Made Millionaires," *Nerdwallet*, March 26, 2014, https://www.nerdwallet.com/blog/finance/8-habits-selfmade-millionaires/.

57. "Better Money Habits Millennial Report," *Bank of America*, 2018, https://bettermoneyhabits.bankofamerica.com/en/millennial-report.

Strange as it sounds, 84% of all millennials in this large sample reported they were "confident" in their ability to manage money, yet 41% of this group also reported feeling financially stressed because they did not have enough savings. In this same study, only 40% of these individuals described themselves as "financially fit" compared with 61% who said they were "physically fit."

In another recent national survey, 69% of millennials reported feeling stressed by financial problems and noted that money was the primary source of their anxiety. Indeed, for a variety of reasons, *Time* magazine says they are the highest-stressed generation today[58].

Savvy financial habits are difficult to learn and can remain challenging throughout life. Young millennials who eat well and get their exercise should practice good financial habits, too. This is the secret of acquiring financial health, so start practicing these habits as early as you can.

In addition to what I've already noted, the following tips can help you develop healthy financial habits and build wealth.

More Wealth-Building Tips

- Your salary isn't enough to build wealth. Make your savings work for you. Generate income from passive investments that accrue over time and keep growing. When I was in my late thirties and earning a lot of money, I took $60,000 I didn't need and bought a fixed annuity from a leading insurance company that was guaranteed to pay 4% interest at a minimum. I still have this annuity, and it's now worth more than half a million dollars and still growing rapidly. As of this writing, bank interest rates are only 1.5%.

---

58. Alexandra Sifferlin, "The Most Stressed-Out Generation? Young Adults," *Time*, February 7, 2013, http://healthland.time.com/2013/02/07/the-most-stressed-out-generation-young-adults/.

- Invest conservatively, start small, and don't lose sleep over it. If you feel insecure about stock investments, look for passive investments that keep the amount of buying and selling to a minimum. Read about smart investing from credible and unbiased financial experts. Read financial newsletters that do not promise "get rich fast" returns. Do not just turn your investments over to financial advisors. Get their returns and know their track records. They earn a lot from their fees, so know what you're paying and hold them accountable. Set financial goals together and track those goals closely. It's your money. Insist your advisors earn it or fire them, regardless of how much you like or trust them. The overwhelming majority of mutual funds do *not* beat the market. Many don't even do as well as the stock market, but stockbrokers make commissions whether you make or lose money from their recommendations. I once had a financial advisor seek to rent an office in a professional building I owned. A quick background report showed he was in debt. Imagine, he was advising other people!

- Build wealth using one or more of the following passive income strategies. 1) Buy a home with a separate guest room or cottage that you can rent out, then use the money to pay down debt or your mortgage. 2) Buy an established franchise that has high returns at a minimal cost such as a Carvel Shop. The city of Westbrook, Connecticut, is home to more than 100 ice cream shops. Northerners love Carvel all year round, and tourists bring in extra summer sales. 3) Buy a business you don't actively manage such as a junkyard for discarded cars and trucks. The used parts net a lucrative return, while the stripped vehicles can be sold for metal and rubber to make room for more vehicles. Hire the right yard manager who knows the parts business and net passive income from selling valuable "junk." 4) Keep an alert eye on profitable companies paying stock dividends such as Apple, which is planning to enter the television industry, and consider investing in them. Imagine your TV sending emails, accessing websites, and more. 5) Put your money to work by offering short-term loans in special situations. For example, builders often take out "bridge" loans to cover their expenses while constructing homes under contract. Banks make interbank loans to one another using investor money available to the public through bond funds currently paying 3%. These funds stay remarkably stable in good or bad markets[59].

- Keep an alert eye on profitable companies such as Apple. In both 2016 and 2017, *Fortune* magazine declared Apple the most profitable company in the world. It completely dominates the smart phone industry with 79% of the world market! That leaves very little room for the many other industry players. Apple plans to further capitalize on its competitive advantage by renting its new iPhones and replacing lost or broken phones for free. Materials from old phones most likely will be recycled, which will further reduce the cost of manufacturing new iPhones. Wow, does this company know how to turn huge profits!

- Buy with an eye to value, not cost. My Mercedes cost a lot, but I've had it for 16 years. This auto is a pearl of a long-term investment. Most cars have to be replaced every six to eight years, but this one holds its value more than twice as long. That's why taxi drivers often drive diesel Mercedes. Most products today aren't meant to last, forcing hapless consumers to buy costly replacements. When you buy furniture, major appliances, or even light bulbs, buy them to last, not just to use.

- Be a wise consumer. The best-selling book *The Millionaire Next Door* shows how people with sensible wealth habits become silent

---

59. John Waggoner, "Be Wary of Bank Loan Funds," *USA Today*, February 13, 2014, https://www.usatoday.com/story/money/columnist/waggoner/2014/02/13/be-wary-of-bank-loan-funds/5457929/.

millionaires[60]. They do not need expensive clothing, fancy vacations, or huge houses. They take vacations and travel, but they are mindful of discounts and special deals and buy wisely at discount stores. In other words, they are not lavish spenders.

- Money traps are everywhere. Watch out for so-called deals on TV. "Buy now, pay later" offers are the worst. If you buy what you can't afford now, you are being set up for a debt trap. In fact, the company hopes you won't be able to pay later; interest and finance charges will then be tacked on to your bill. Gotcha! As mentioned, watch out for credit card debt and also for companies on TV that want to help you "consolidate" your credit card debts into one simple payment. If you're considering this, you're already trapped. Find a reputable public service agency that can advise you before stepping into the credit card mousetrap.

- Smart investing is no different than smart buying. Stay within your means. Some investors borrow from brokerage houses to increase their bets on certain stocks. If you can't afford a lot of the stock, brokerage houses offer to buy stock "on margin." In other words, you borrow money from them and pay only a little bit for the stock upfront. If it increases markedly, you win and can cash in and pay your stock loan. If the stock goes down markedly, your broker will call in your loan and you'll be forced to sell the stock to pay your debt for the loan. I call this "the greed trap," and it can happen quickly if the stock suddenly drops a lot. Wealth lesson: do not buy stock you cannot afford to lose.

- Buy smart all the time, no matter your age. At a discount upscale clothing company, I recently bought a high-end leather belt that was

---

60. "The Millionaire Next Door," *Wikipedia*, last modified September 16, 2017, https://en.wikipedia.org/wiki/The_Millionaire_Next_Door, accessed April 9, 2018.

marked down almost 75%! Men's belts don't go out of style, so this was a good buy. What's more, I noticed a rep handing out coupons for $5.00 to customers as they left the store. I made a mental note, and when I went to pay for the belt, I mentioned that a sales rep was giving out coupons to people as they left the store. Though I hadn't yet left, I asked if I could have the discount anyway, and the answer was yes! Just asking was enough to get the savings!

- Never assume the asking price is the price you have to pay. Everyone knows you don't pay the asking price for a new car. In fact, websites will tell you how much the dealer paid for the car he's selling. On smaller items, most people don't think twice about simply paying. At large stores, the price is the price, but it doesn't hurt to ask for a discount, especially if you're buying several expensive items. Sometimes you can find Internet or catalogue sales on items you want to buy at the store. It never hurts to ask. I once bought an expensive gold chain at a large retail store. It was marked down, and the sales clerk asked if I had a Preferred Card issued with the company. I said I'd had one a few years ago, and she looked for the card in her computer system but couldn't find it. I explained that the card had been issued in another store located in another state. She gave me the better price simply because I gave her a plausible explanation.

- Bargain for the price you want to pay at small outdoor concessions, flea markets, garage sales, consignment shops, and so on. Most people are uncomfortable doing this, but get used to it! The owner is never going to take less than the product's wholesale price. Bargain low but not ridiculously low. In one instance, the owner said he couldn't take less, but if I paid cash, I wouldn't have to pay the sales tax. I suspected he wasn't going to report the sale, but no matter. I saved money.

- Be savvy when buying a car. Before stepping into an auto dealership, do your homework! Consider buying a "used" or "pre-owned" car.

As soon as a new car is sold and driven off the lot, it depreciates 20–25% depending on the make and model. Cars that are almost new are sometimes returned because the leaser couldn't make the payments. Other individuals sell their almost-new cars because they can't afford them. Some auto rental companies sell their cars after two or so years, many with low mileage. Buying an almost-new car is smart buying, especially if you can afford to pay cash. If you have the savings, avoiding car debt is definitely the way to go.

- Be savvy when buying a house or condominium. Few people can afford to pay with cash, which makes shopping around for the best mortgage rate a must. Know the hidden costs of mortgages, including fees and closing costs. In a slow housing market, you might get a realtor to absorb some of the fees. Better yet is a direct purchase from an owner or builder that allows you to bypass realtor fees. If you don't know the real estate market, a realtor can be an excellent resource; just keep in mind this person is a salesperson and earns fees from both the buyer and the seller. Make certain you get "comps" and learn what comparable homes in your area are selling for. Also, be prepared to bargain. If the seller can't agree to your desired price, try to get other breaks to sweeten the deal. I remember when my home wasn't moving in a slow housing market. Finally, I got a low offer. Both the buyer and I had realtors, and I persuaded both realtors to discount their fees to move the sale forward. Always think creatively on large purchases.

- When you buy a home, take a 15-year rather than a 30-year mortgage if you can afford the higher payments because the total cost of this mortgage can save you thousands of dollars. If your mortgage is the more common 30-year type, insist on a clause that allows you to accelerate your payments at no charge. You never know when your income might unexpectedly jump and an opportunity to pay down your mortgage appears. In my view, the sooner you stop making mortgage payments, the faster you can save money and build passive wealth.

Money mistakes are common. You might spend a lot for a product that's cheaper online. You might take out a small loan for an expense that can't be paid off early without paying the full interest on the loan. I once invested in a "penny stock" a broker sold me cheaply. Within a week, he'd sold it for a net gain of $3,000. I bought another penny stock with my profit for another quick gain. Feeling upbeat, I bought two more penny stocks and quickly lost $10,000 about as fast as I'd made $5,000. Yes, I lost five grand in only a few weeks. I was a naïve investor. I had no knowledge of the financial soundness of these companies or their markets, and—I admit it—I'd been caught in the "greed trap."

Wealth lesson: invest blindly, and you will get hurt. Con artists lurk everywhere, and even wealthy investors get burned. As a rule of thumb, if a financial company promises you unrealistic returns, even if it delivers for a while, watch out! People have lost their entire life savings this way.

In sum, here are my wisdoms about wealth-building habits:

- Financial skills are best learned early in life. If you don't have enough money to get everything you want, count yourself fortunate. You will learn to respect money much more if you don't have everything you ever dreamed of. Wealthy parents have to work especially hard to get their children to learn good saving habits and to respect the value of money. Don't ever take money for granted. It can slip through your fingers.

- No one gets through life without making financial mistakes. Most mistakes happen because you haven't done your homework or have been tempted by greed. Credit cards are an invitation to go into debt. Don't buy what you can't afford. Ask yourself what you can do without and make a habit of saving regularly. If you can't save, you can't afford what you're buying. You must spend less or earn more. Most of us waste money and don't realize how it slips away. Keep very close tabs on your saving and buying habits.

- Few people get wealthy from their own salaries. Use passive income to build wealth and be patient as it grows. Invest wisely and keep

- tabs on your investments. If you use other experts to invest your money, watch their returns closely. Never lose sight of your financial portfolio.

- Be frugal even if you're wealthy. Learn to hate waste. Buy things with value in mind. Built-to-last products are wealth builders, especially for large costly items.

- Don't be afraid to bargain. No one is going to give you something under cost unless they're desperate to sell. There's always a rock-bottom price below which the seller won't go. Remember, to save money, you don't need to make ridiculous offers. Stay low but off rock bottom. Buy smart and look for coupons, discounts, and special sales whenever you can.

- Live beneath your means. Get out of debt as soon as you can. Use passive income to accrue wealth. Be patient. Wealth building starts slowly but builds rapidly as you save more and income compounds.

- Enjoy the ride. Invest to build a portfolio from different passive sources, and watch your wealth grow faster well into your retirement years.

Recommended Readings

Internet References

"Better Money Habits Millennial Report." *Bank of America*, 2018. https://bettermoneyhabits.bankofamerica.com/en/millennial-report.

Cussen, Mark P. "Money Habits of the Millennials." *Investopedia*, June 30, 2017. https://www.investopedia.com/articles/personal-finance/021914/money-habits-millennials.asp.

"How to Build Wealth." *WikiHow*, 2018. https://www.wikihow.com/Build-Wealth.

Sifferlin, Alexandra. "The Most Stressed-Out Generation? Young Adults." *Time*, Feburary 7, 2013. http://healthland.time.com/2013/02/07/the-most-stressed-out-generation-young-adults/.

"The Millionaire Next Door." *Wikipedia*, last modified September 16, 2017. https://en.wikipedia.org/wiki/The_Millionaire_Next_Door, accessed April 9, 2018.

Voigt, Kevin. "8 Habits of Self-Made Millionaires." *Nerdwallet*, March 26, 2014. https://www.nerdwallet.com/blog/finance/8-habits-selfmade-millionaires/.

Waggoner, John. "Be Wary of Bank Loan Funds." *USA Today*, February 13, 2014. https://www.usatoday.com/story/money/columnist/waggoner/2014/02/13/be-wary-of-bank-loan-funds/5457929/.

Print References

Wertheimer, Neil. "Lessons from the Rich." *AARP The Magazine*. Feb.–March 2017, 60 (2c), 98.

SECTION IV:

Life Skills to Achieve Your Full Potential

Chapter 15:

Happiness

THERE IS NO GUARANTEED FORMULA for happiness, though just about everyone has studied, researched, and written books about it. Want a scientific explanation of what happens in your brain when you're happy?

That explanation exists.

Want a psychological definition of what happens when people are happy?

That definition exists.

My point is, only you can know what makes you happy. Being happy is a challenge throughout life, in part because what makes you happy changes at different stages of life and even on a daily basis.

An easier question to answer is, "What makes you unhappy?" Even then, what makes one person unhappy does not necessarily make another person unhappy. However, as a psychologist, I have helped some very unhappy people. Some didn't believe they were worthwhile. Others were scared to death they might fail. Still others *had* failed, sometimes repeatedly, and didn't know how to change. I'll bet you've been unhappy with a grade that disappointed you or with a friend, parent, romantic partner, or employer. I could go on and on about what makes people unhappy.

A more important question to ask, one that will help you gain greater wisdom, is, "What might you try to do when you're unhappy?" Its ancillary question, "What are you willing to try?", is just as important.

I suggest you put your resourcefulness to work to answer these questions. You can ask other people to help you, but don't be surprised if you can't or don't want to accept their advice. Even if you do listen to their suggestions, remember that you can't copy other people's wisdom. Their advice simply might not be right for you.

Once you discover what makes you happy, engage in this activity or passion as often as you can, but keep adding new experiences to your life's menu all the time. Don't let your menu get stale. Sometimes you'll just fall into something you enjoy, but at other times, you'll have to search for new and intriguing things to do. About all I can say is, prepare to push yourself to your maximum if you want to create a full and rewarding life, but be prepared for low times in spite of your best efforts.

There's no magic formula for happiness, though the search for happiness and the experience of being unhappy do lead to some valuable life lessons. One is to stay active and interested in the things that surround you. If you get too comfortable with life, you can lose interest in venturing out to experience the world. Soon you'll be bored and unproductive. Two, help other people and give back to them in your own way. Isolation is a sure way to be unhappy. Three, learn something new every day and make learning a lifelong habit. If you don't, your brain might slow down and you might grow tired of living. Don't become a couch potato as I did when my wife was sick. Living, learning, and experiencing is how you develop self-understanding and wisdom. Four, when you're unhappy, be resourceful. Don't let unhappiness get the best of you.

I hope you fall in love, maybe even more than once. You can get along without love, but you'll miss out on one of life's great pleasures. As mentioned, married people are happier than others. Of course, suffering in a bad marriage without love is painful and emotionally depleting and a sure prescription for unhappiness.

The brain is a remarkable organ. When I asked adults in my practice to think back on their lives and tell me when they were most happy, many couldn't come up with one single moment, but when I asked when they were most unhappy, they could sift through their many experiences and find that one time quickly.

Storing and then retrieving hurtful and even terrible life experiences from our memory banks is how the brain protects us and even helps us become more mentally tough. While certain individuals "repress" or forget painful experiences, healthy adults are very much aware of the terrible parts of their lives. However, they find it much harder to recall the happiest times. When my clients finally did so, I was able to help them discover aspects of their own healthy personalities they didn't recognize or see very clearly.

Remember, understanding yourself is the basis of all wisdom. I encourage you, when you reach midlife, to pause and ask yourself when you were most happy and when you were least happy. Then, examine your answers very carefully for the wisdom they can yield about how you might optimally live your life going forward.

The happiest time in my life came when I was 24 years old and attending graduate school in a beautiful state far from where I'd grown up. I'd married just two years earlier and was deeply in love. My wife joined me and began graduate school, too. We both thoroughly enjoyed meeting other graduate students and professors from all over the country. It was spring, with flowers blooming everywhere. Sometimes we took breakfast picnics with our new university friends to the nearby national park. Sometimes we just got in the car and drove wherever we wanted, exploring new places. One time we came across something called the gravity shack. An enterprising guy had built it to defy gravity, or so he claimed. My wife and I decided to pay his fee and give it a try. Upon entering the shack, we found ourselves going up, down, sideways, in all different directions. Completely disoriented, we laughed our heads off and hugged each other in pure joy.

You don't have to be a psychologist to understand why I was so happy. I was young, healthy, in love, enjoying my classes, meeting interesting people, exploring new places with my beautiful wife, and preparing to enter a professional practice I knew I would enjoy. It didn't matter that we had very little money. We even laughed about finding creative ways to eat on the cheap!

Barry M. Cohen, PhD

The most unhappy time in my life came when I was 40 years old and very busy with my career and raising a family when we suddenly received news that my healthy wife had ovarian cancer that was beginning to spread. That led to a full year of chemotherapy resulting in hair loss, vomiting, physical weakness, and worse as the drugs attacked the cancer cells but also other healthy cells. Then the doctors took "a second look" to see if the cancer cells were gone. Well, some still lingered. Ovarian cancer death rates were high, and we knew the odds weren't good. No doctor or hospital in our area could help us, so we decided to go to New York City to consult with doctors who specialized in advanced treatments to fight this disease.

One famous doctor recommended chemotherapy via a cocktail of three highly powerful drugs that could cause serious harm to my wife's already weakened body. We also were offered an experimental treatment given right at the site of the disease and delivered through a surgically implanted port. There was no guarantee of success, and we'd have to fly to the medical center for treatment every month for six months.

We chose the experimental option, and I closed my practice for the duration of the treatment. On our first trip, I delivered my wife to hospital admissions and went to park the car. The hospital was so busy that I was forced to park on the street. I opened the trunk, removed some things my wife needed, and headed into the hospital to join her. When I got back to the car, I discovered all our luggage had been stolen! I remember standing there feeling helpless, grieving and worrying about what would happen next in my life. I felt very alone.

Miraculously, my wife beat the disease. My life and career started anew. Soon, I was busier than ever, and our kids were thrilled their lives hadn't been turned upside down. Funny how life works… Sometimes when things look very grim and you think the worst will happen, it doesn't. At such times, you just bounce back and begin where you left off.

We were very lucky. Many patients who took the experimental treatment didn't survive, but we didn't give up, even when we were both down. The lesson: cherish life and keep going, no matter what. Take risks but don't be reckless. Keep your head up and forge ahead. Hopefully, you'll be lucky in life, too.

Our great forefathers who created the Declaration of Independence wrote that the pursuit of happiness is a very great American freedom and the right of all citizens. Of course, some people confuse happiness with satisfaction.

I'm not asking if you're satisfied. If you're content with life, are free of pain, and are comfortable, you're probably satisfied. That's not the same as being happy.

When you're happy, you laugh like a kid, intrigued and curious about all life can offer. Your brain is nourished as you laugh, and you do so easily and often.

Of course, I don't expect you to always be happy. Your jumble of experiences will range from unhappiness to contentment to sheer joy. But if wisdom is all about understanding yourself, knowing what makes you happy will strengthen your wisdom muscles. That's why, in addition to asking yourself at midlife when you were most happy and most unhappy, I encourage you to ask yourself once a year, "Am I happy now?"

Psychologist Martin Seligman has devoted his entire professional career to studying happiness[61]. His central finding is that happiness isn't related to external events such as winning the lottery or taking a once-in-a-lifetime vacation. Such events quickly wear off and we go back to feeling exactly as we felt before. Instead, happiness is largely related to character strength and internal qualities.

According to Seligman, happy individuals feel appreciation and gratitude for what they have. They report feelings of hope and zest. They love and feel loved. They're also blessed with social support from good friends.

If you're unhappy, it's time to take stock and get resourceful about improving or changing your life. Maybe just making a small change will do

---

61. Dorothy Foltz-Gray, "What Makes Us Happy?" *Prevention*, November 3, 2011, https://www.prevention.com/mind-body/emotional-health/what-makes-us-happy.

the trick. I knew a couple with kids and a busy schedule whose relationship was going stale until they decided to start going out to dinner together once a week. By making time for themselves, they found greater joy. Many busy adults get so wrapped up in their hectic lives that they lose the joy they once felt. Some say they're much too busy to think about happiness, but that's just an excuse for not doing the hard thinking to apply some ingenuity to enrich their lives.

It might intrigue you to know that the brain can experience enjoyable places and events without the body being present. In so doing, it creates happiness. Remember those mirror neurons in your brain? They help you have fun just by seeing others having fun! A recent innovation in prison life came after authorities realized that bored inmates who became unruly just to enliven their bland existence behaved better after watching videos of people doing extraordinary things like taking a helicopter ride over the Grand Canyon or surfing huge waves in Hawaii[62].

One of Disney's most popular rides used to be called Soarin' Over California. Even wheelchair-bound people loved this ride! You sat down, were lifted just a few feet into the air, and then a fantastic video began. You saw clouds in the sky that opened up right before your eyes. You had the immediate sensation of flying over the Golden Gate Bridge and then Yosemite Park. You whizzed over majestic snow-covered mountains and flew over the brilliantly lit Disney Park in Los Angeles. This ride only lifted you two feet off the ground, yet you were truly soaring!

This ride was so popular that Disney recently replaced it with Soarin' Around the World in an effort to appeal to more visitors. Magnificent destinations now include the Eiffel Tower and the Great Wall of China. The scenery might have changed, but the happiness people experience mimics

---

62. "Prison in Washington State Is Latest to Institute 'Blue Room,'" *Correctional News*, September 9, 2015, http://correctionalnews.com/2015/09/09/prison-in-washington-state-latest-institute-blue-room/.

the happiness they felt on the original ride because the brain loves these experiences no matter where it happens to be soaring!

Built for happiness, the brain is an amazing organ. Just give it the opportunity to work for you. There are many ways to reduce stress and find relaxation. People who meditate sometimes reach a state of complete relaxation and inner peace, but even this isn't happiness.

We are each capable of happiness, of feelings of pure joy, and even laughter that bursts out and makes us cry. When I experienced the happiest time in my life, my brain was constantly nourished by several rewarding things all happening simultaneously. I was in love, I was healthy, and my brain cells were firing a mile a minute. You might say all cylinders were working together!

In sum, here are my happiness wisdoms:

- No one can tell you how to be happy. It's up to you to make your life happy and to work to keep it that way.

- Really bad experiences can and do happen. If you can tough them out, life will get better. New flowers come up all the time.

- People get into funks all the time. Ask yourself once every year if you're happy. Take stock and don't mistake or accept contentment as happiness.

- Get resourceful if you want to change your life. Think out of the box and find fresh ways to live and pursue joy.

- Make happiness, not career success, the standard by which you judge yourself and the gold standard for every stage of your life. You might find you're unhappy with parts of your life while other parts of your life are a lot of fun. If you want to add more happiness to your life, you can try to change or eliminate the bad stuff, but it probably won't go away easily or quickly. Instead, try accepting what you can't change and use your energy to create new life experiences you completely enjoy. Your brain will reward you as you enrich your life!

Barry M. Cohen, PhD

Recommended Readings

Internet References

Aaker, Jennifer, and Smith, Emily Esfahani. "Not Everyone Wants to Be Happy." *Scientific American*, October 28, 2014. https://www.scientificamerican.com/article/not-everyone-wants-to-be-happy/.

Becker, Joshua. "10 Positive Psychological Studies to Change Your View of Happiness." *Becoming Minimalist*, May 22, 2014, https://www.becomingminimalist.com/happier/.

Foltz-Gray, Dorothy. "What Makes Us Happy?" *Prevention*, November 3, 2011. https://www.prevention.com/mind-body/emotional-health/what-makes-us-happy.

"Happiness." *Changing Minds*, 2018. www.changingminds.org/explanations/emotions/happiness.

"Prison in Washington State Is Latest to Institute 'Blue Room.'" *Correctional News*, September 9, 2015. http://correctionalnews.com/2015/09/09/prison-in-washington-state-latest-institute-blue-room/.

Chapter 16:

Smart Aging

IN THE 1600S, THE AVERAGE life expectancy was 30 years. In 2012, the average life expectancy was nearly 79 years[63]. Human beings are living longer for many reasons, including better public health practices such as effective sanitation, clean water, and improved personal hygiene as well as significant advances in nutrition and medicine. Some scientists doubt the average life expectancy will increase beyond 90 years, but others say vastly higher life spans are possible if science can crack the causes of aging.

One cause of aging is oxidative stress, caused when highly reactive substances called oxidants damage our DNA as well as the proteins in our bodies and our fat cells[64]. We produce some oxidants normally when we breathe, but other oxidants are caused by infections and inflammation. Consuming too much alcohol and smoking cigarettes increases oxidants, which is why abusing these addictive substances causes aging.

---

63. Laura Helmuth, "Why Are You Not Dead Yet?" *Slate*, September 5, 2013, http://www.slate.com/articles/health_and_science/science_of_longevity/2013/09/life_expectancy_history_public_health_and_medical_advances_that_lead_to.html.

64. "Understanding Oxidative Stress," *Waller Wellness Center*, 2018, https://www.wallerwellness.com/what-is-functional-medicine/understanding-oxidative-stress.

In one study, scientists exposed worms to two substances that neutralized oxidants. These worms lived almost twice as long as untreated worms![65] Maybe scientists will break through the upper limits of aging just by controlling the oxidants in our bodies.

Another cause of aging occurs when glucose, the main ingredient in the sugar we use as energy, binds to some of the DNA, proteins, and fat cells in our bodies, causing them to be unable to do their jobs[66]. The problem gets worse as we get older. Eventually, it causes our tissues to become diseased and die.

Speaking of sugar, government nutrition guidelines restrict these sweet soluble carbohydrates, but people of all ages love carbonated drinks, candy, and chocolate. Tellingly, though our taste buds lose sensitivity as we age, our ability to taste sugar is pretty much the last thing to go. Simultaneously, studies on animals show that eating a reduced diet can lead to greater longevity[67]. While more research is needed on humans, it seems prudent to eat less sugar, and maybe less food altogether, as we age. Adults simply don't need the same number of calories that growing bodies

---

65. Natalie Kalin, "Immortality May Be More Than Mere Fiction," *Huff Post*, February 6, 2017, https://www.huffingtonpost.com/natalie-kalin/immortality-may-be-more-t_b_9178214.html.

66. Joseph Mercola, "Avoid Sugar to Help Slow Aging," *Mercola*, February 22, 2012, https://articles.mercola.com/sites/articles/archive/2012/02/22/how-sugar-accelerates-aging.aspx.

67. Richard Conniff, "The Hunger Gains: Extreme Calorie-Restriction Diet Shows Anti-Aging Results," *Scientific American*, February 16, 2017, https://www.scientificamerican.com/article/the-hunger-gains-extreme-calorie-restriction-diet-shows-anti-aging-results/.

require[68]. Seniors need even fewer calories, which is why some restaurants offer menus suited just for them.

Good genes makes a difference in how we age, too. Studies show that 20%–30% of a person's life expectancy is due to inherited genes[69]. That means a good 70%–80% of our life span is up to us and the choices we make. In other words, if you make smart lifestyle choices, you can live longer. The choice isn't between quantity (long life) and quality (healthy living). Good health is a must for living longer. Even if you inherit bad genes, a healthy life will extend your years.

We're always aging, no matter how old we are. The important question is, what smart aging practices can we control that extend life? You might not have any warning such as pain, discomfort, disease, or weakness, but starting somewhere between ages 30 and 40, your body will start wearing down. In fact, everything on the planet eventually wears out. Scientists call this physical phenomenon the Law of Entropy.

You can slow your body's aging process by following smart aging practices, including those listed below[70,71]. I suggest you begin and keep at them well before you reach middle age!

---

68. Robert Roy Britt, "Live Longer: The One Anti-Aging Trick That Works," *Live Science*, July 8, 2008, https://www.livescience.com/2666-live-longer-anti-aging-trick-works.html.

69. Giuseppe Passarino, Frecesco De Rango, and Alberto Montesanto, "Human Longevity: Genetics or Lifestyle? It Takes Two to Tango," *Immun Ageing: I & A 13* (2016): 12, April 5, 2016, https://www.ncbi.nlm.nih.gov/pmc/articles/PMC4822264/.

70. J. Kluger, "Get Your Head Out of the Game," *Time*, 2015, 185, 83–86.

71. M. Oaklander, "Stretch Your Time Line," *Time*, 2015, 185, 80–81.

Your skin. Your skin is the first organ to age. To keep it healthy, you need to be vigilant early in life and remain vigilant as you grow older. Collagen and stretchy elastin decline about 1% a year starting at age 18. Teens don't notice this slow decline, but it happens to all of us.

To slow the decline, eat well, avoid cigarettes, and wear sunscreen whenever you go outdoors. Teens who love to sunbathe and tan should know that the sun is the biggest threat to their skin; water reflecting off oceans and lakes causes the rays of the sun to be even more harmful. Sunscreens have to be reapplied every four hours or they are useless, and damage from a bad burn in your teens can show up many years later as skin cancer.

Sure enough, when I was in my forties, I discovered a form of skin cancer called squamous cell carcinoma on my back caused by sunburns I'd gotten as a teen. My doctor was able to remove this tissue, and now I see my doctor annually and also regularly inspect my own skin for anything that looks suspicious. Learn what the early signs of skin cancer look like and inspect yourself everywhere, especially your toes and ears.

Your lungs. By age 30, lung capacity starts to decline. The antidote for strong lungs is exercise. Sedentary people lose up to 1% of their lung capacity a year.

Your bones. By age 35, bone density starts to decline 1% a year. Weight-bearing exercise helps a lot, but walking or even jumping in place every day helps, too.

Your muscles. By age 40, you must start exercising or you will lose muscle and gain fat.

Your brain. After age 70, age-related changes start to speed up. Brain games will *not* help memory loss[72]. Stick to activities that stimulate and engage you. Watching television isn't one of them!

Your hearing. Age-related hearing loss happens gradually. Listening to very loud music hastens it. By age 65–74, one-third of individuals have some hearing loss.

---

72. J. Worland, "Can Brain Games Keep My Mind Young?" *Time*, 2015, 185, 87.

Your heart. As we age, the walls of the heart get thicker and the arteries get stiffer. Heart aerobic capacity peaks between ages 20 and 30 and drops about 10% every 10 years. Good nutrition and exercise can ward off heart disease, which usually begins for people age 65 or older.

Your kidneys. You probably won't feel it, but by age 50, the kidneys start to decline. Drinking lots of water helps. The problem is, thirst decreases with age. We all should make a habit of drinking lots of water, even when we're not thirsty!

According to the World Health Organization, the leading cause of death worldwide is cardiovascular disease, which accounts for three of every 10 deaths, including ischemic heart attacks and strokes. In countries with high incomes, seven of 10 deaths for people over 70 years of age are caused by cardiovascular diseases, cancers, dementia, diabetes, and chronic obstructive lung disease[73].

You can reduce your chances of developing these conditions with sound nutritional practices, by exercising regularly, by staying active and involved, and by not smoking or abusing alcohol.

Other smart practices that will help you stay healthy and slow the aging process involve the following psychological remedies and lifestyle changes:

- Live in a healthy environment that's "age smart" with easy access to medical care and cultural stimulation. Cities with these advantages also typically have low crime rates, pedestrian-friendly gathering places, accessible transportation, educational enrichment programs, and clean air. In 2015, of the 100 top places to live in the United States, the city of Madison, Wisconsin, came in first[74]. It has all the advantages for age-smart living, but there are many other good

---

73. "The Top 10 Causes of Death," *World Health Organization*, January 2017, www.who.int/mediacentre/factsheets/fs310/en.

74. J. Worland, "Can Brain Games Keep My Mind Young?" *Time*, 2015, 185, 87.

choices as well. Naples, Florida, was ranked the "Happiest Place in America" in 2015 and 2016[75]. If you want to savor a social life among people who enjoy themselves, eat healthy, and exercise in a warm gulf-side beach community, this is it!

- Practice mindfulness-based stress reduction. This means learning to meditate and paying close attention to your feelings and thoughts while staying in the present. In other words, learn to calm your body and mind. Some studies suggest meditation can calm inflamed immune systems[76], while brain studies show age-related gray matter decline can be slowed[77]. Yet another study shows that transcendental meditation can slow the effects of aging. One study even found that just eight hours of meditation decreased the genes that regulate inflammation.

- Sleep well and get enough rest. The magic number of recommended hours is seven, according to medical doctors[78]. During restful sleep, neurons busily pulse over, in rhythmic order, ensuring that the brain's hormones, enzymes, and proteins are in good working order. Meanwhile, toxic fluids are washed out that can cause all kinds of problems, including premature brain aging and even early onset

---

75. Brigit Katz, "Is This the Happiest Place in America?" *Smithsonian*, March 7, 2017, https://www.smithsonianmag.com/smart-news/happiest-place-america-180962416/.

76. Seth Segall and David S. Black, "Can Meditation Slow the Aging Process?" *American Society on Aging*, March 4, 2014, asaging.org/blog/can-meditation-slow-aging-process.

77. Ibid.

78. Alice Park, "The Sleep Cure," *Time*, 2017, 189, 70–76.

Alzheimer's disease. Researchers have found that restful sleep enhances creativity, learning, and memory while too little sleep causes mental and physical fatigue and diminishes your ability to perform high-level cognitive tasks.

- Stay positive and surround yourself with others who are positive. Research shows that even mildly optimistic people live longer than pessimists[79], so choose a non-toxic social environment. People who live harmoniously slow the aging process!

- Help those who are less fortunate than you. Volunteering provides a sense of purpose and a "helper's high" due to the release of endorphins after a kind or generous act.

- Dietary supplements do *not* appear to slow aging, but eating fewer calories as you age does increase longevity, as long as you're getting your minerals and vitamins. Drinking alcohol in moderation can also significantly increase life expectancy.

- Eat your fruits and vegetables! In a study of Seventh-day Adventists who consumed a vegetarian diet, men lived an astonishing nine and a half years longer and women six years longer than the general population[80]. Their spirituality might have played a role, too, since studies show it reduces the stress that shortens life.

---

79. Anna Hodgekiss, "Optimists DO Live Longer: Looking on the Bright Side of Life 'Halves the Risk of Heart Problems," *Daily Mail*, January 14, 2015, http://www.dailymail.co.uk/health/article-2909933/Optimists-live-longer-Looking-bright-life-means-likely-heart-problems.html.

80. Liz Rowley, "Do Vegetarians Live Longer? Here's What Science Says," *Mic*, February 10, 2016, https://mic.com/articles/134825/do-vegetarians-live-longer-heres-what-science-says#.SUrrypGo1.

A significant breakthrough in aging won two scientists the Nobel Prize in Medicine in 1978 when they discovered an enzyme called telomerase that maintains and repairs telomeres[81,82]. Telomeres keep chromosomes from fraying or sticking to each other and consequently scrambling or even destroying genetic material. Alas, when cells divide, telomeres get shorter. When they get too short, cells die or become inactive. This shortening process is associated with aging, cancer, and a higher risk of death.

Now, evidence is mounting that telomeres get shorter in response to great stress.

In a study of women with severe stress caused by the death of a child, divorce, unemployment, financial loss, or family conflict, the greater the stress, the shorter their telomeres became. However, women in this sample who practiced good health behaviors such as resting, sleeping well, eating healthy, and exercising managed to maintain their telomere length! In another study, telomere damage occurred largely in individuals who were sedentary.

A landmark study on newborns conducted shortly after birth tested their cord blood and telomere lengths. Remarkably, babies who experienced easy deliveries had longer telomeres than babies who had difficult deliveries[83]. It appears that healthy telomere lengths do not start at birth but in fact start before we are born.

---

81. Law Wing Sze, "How Can We Slow the Ageing Process?" *British Council*, April 24, 2015, britishcouncil.org/voices-magazine/how-can-we-slow-ageing-process.

82. "How to Lengthen Your Telomeres and Unlock the Key to Longevity," *Dr. Axe*, 2018, https://draxe.com/telomeres/.

83. Siew-Peng Lee, Prakash Hande, George SH Yeo, and Ene-Choo Tan, "Correlation of Cord Blood Telomere Length with Birth Weight," *BMC Res Notes* 10 (2017): 469, September 8, 2017, https://www.ncbi.nlm.nih.gov/pmc/articles/PMC5591543/.

Can telomerase supplements or artificially manufactured telomerase maintain telomere length and hold back aging? Regretfully, no. Only healthy behaviors appear to increase telomerase and extend telomere length.

No one knows for certain if telomeres will unlock the keys to extending life, but scientists do know that reducing stress and engaging in healthy behaviors increases longevity. Perhaps telomeres will merely become a biomarker for healthy living. Then again, perhaps telomeres will eventually extend longevity, assuming we can modify their lengths to protect our aging genes.

In sum, here are my wisdoms for smart aging:

- Everything on earth ages and eventually dies. Aging is a natural process. Every organ in our bodies ages, but certain organs begin this process sooner than others. Unhealthy practices cause organs to age faster than they otherwise would.

- You can do a lot to slow the aging process of your organs. For example, your skin begins to age starting at around age 18. Teens love the beach and outdoor sports and games, but they should protect their skin with sunscreens. A bad burn can show up as skin cancer years later. Don't take chances with your skin!

- There are two main causes of aging: inflammation in your body and oxidants or highly reactive substances that attack your DNA, proteins, and fat cells. Smoking, disease, infections, and alcohol abuse accelerate these aging processes.

- Don't count on "good genes" to keep you from aging. If you're blessed with good genes, count yourself lucky, but genes only account for 20%–30% of the aging process. The rest is up to the lifestyle choices you make.

- Vegetarians live longer than other people. Eat your fruits and vegetables!

- Stay active and engaged all your life. Keep moving and exercise regularly. These are the keys to aging slowly.

- Meditation is a terrific way to reduce stress and has been proven to extend longevity.

- Cut back on your calories and the amount of food you consume as you get older. Most of us eat more than we need. Unless you have health problems or a high metabolic rate, eating less as you age is wise.

- As you get older, give serious thought to where you want to reside. Smart-aging communities boast quality-of-life factors that promote healthy aging.

- Stress-reduction strategies will enhance your emotional and physical health. They also help you maintain telomeres and even increase their length. Telomeres might be the next medical breakthrough because they hold our genetic material together and prevent our cells from dying or becoming inactive.

- If you make smart aging decisions, you will increase your chances of living longer *and* you will drastically improve the quality of your life. The younger you start, the greater your chances of living a long, healthy life.

Recommended Readings

Internet References

Britt, Robert Roy. "Live Longer: The One Anti-Aging Trick That Works." *Live Science*, July 8, 2008. https://www.livescience.com/2666-live-longer-anti-aging-trick-works.html.

Conniff, Richard. "The Hunger Gains: Extreme Calorie-Restriction Diet Shows Anti-Aging Results." *Scientific American*, February 16, 2017. https://www.scientificamerican.com/article/the-hunger-gains-extreme-calorie-restriction-diet-shows-anti-aging-results/.

Helmuth, Laura. "Why Are You Not Dead Yet?" *Slate*, September 5, 2013. http://www.slate.com/articles/health_and_science/science_of_longevity/2013/09/life_expectancy_history_public_health_and_medical_advances_that_lead_to.html.

Hodgekiss, Anna. "Optimists DO Live Longer: Looking on the Bright Side of Life 'Halves the Risk of Heart Problems." *Daily Mail*, January 14, 2015. http://www.dailymail.co.uk/health/article-2909933/Optimists-live-longer-Looking-bright-life-means-likely-heart-problems.html.

"How to Lengthen Your Telomeres and Unlock the Key to Longevity." *Dr. Axe*, 2018. https://draxe.com/telomeres/.

Kalin, Natalie. "Immortality May Be More Than Mere Fiction." *Huff Post*, February 6, 2017. https://www.huffingtonpost.com/natalie-kalin/immortality-may-be-more-t_b_9178214.html.

Katz, Brigit. "Is This the Happiest Place in America?" *Smithsonian*, March 7, 2017. https://www.smithsonianmag.com/smart-news/happiest-place-america-180962416/.

Lee, Siew-Peng, Hande, Prakash, Yeo, George SH, and Tan, Ene-Choo. "Correlation of Cord Blood Telomere Length with Birth Weight." *BMC Res Notes* 10 (2017): 469, September 8, 2017. https://www.ncbi.nlm.nih.gov/pmc/articles/PMC5591543/.

Mercola, Joseph. "Avoid Sugar to Help Slow Aging." *Mercola*, February 22, 2012. https://articles.mercola.com/sites/articles/archive/2012/02/22/how-sugar-accelerates-aging.aspx.

"Naples, Florida, Remains Top US Metro for Well-Being." *Well-Being Index*, March 6, 2017. https://wellbeingindex.sharecare.com/naples-top-metro-well-being/.

Passarino, Giuseppe, De Rango, Frecesco, and Montesanto, Alberto. "Human Longevity: Genetics or Lifestyle? It Takes Two to Tango."

Immun Ageing: I & A 13 (2016): 12, April 5, 2016. https://www.ncbi.nlm.nih.gov/pmc/articles/PMC4822264/.

Rowley, Liz. "Do Vegetarians Live Longer? Here's What Science Says." *Mic*, February 10, 2016. https://mic.com/articles/134825/do-vegetarians-live-longer-heres-what-science-says#.SUrrypGo1.

Segall, Seth, and Black, David S. "Can Meditation Slow the Aging Process?" *American Society on Aging*, March 4, 2014. asaging.org/blog/can-meditation-slow-aging-process.

Sze, Law Wing. "How Can We Slow the Ageing Process?" *British Council*, April 24, 2015. britishcouncil.org/voices-magazine/how-can-we-slow-ageing-process.

"The Top 10 Causes of Death." *World Health Organization*, January 2017. http://www.who.int/mediacentre/factsheets/fs310/en/.

"Understanding Oxidative Stress." *Waller Wellness Center*, 2018. https://www.wallerwellness.com/what-is-functional-medicine/understanding-oxidative-stress.

Wise, Abigail. "7 Habits of People Who Age Well." *Real Simple*, 2018. https://www.realsimple.com/health/preventative-health/habits-of-people-who-age-well.

Print References

Kluger, J. "Get Your Head Out of the Game." *Time*. 2015, 185, 83–86.

Oaklander, M. "Stretch Your Time Line." *Time*. 2015, 185, 80–81.

Park, Alice. "The Sleep Cure." *Time*. 2017, 189, 70–76.

Worland, J. "Can Brain Games Keep My Mind Young?" *Time*. 2015, 185, 87.

Worland, J. "What Is the Best Place to Be an Old Person?" *Time*. 2015, 185, 79.

Chapter 17:

Self-Fulfillment and Beyond

I WAS BORN IN 1943, the same year Abraham Maslow published his famous "hierarchy of needs"[84]. Maslow knew that all individuals could achieve wisdom, but he noted that people whose basic needs were met had greater opportunities to acquire wisdom *and* to reach their full potential.

What were the basic needs Maslow believed people needed to satisfy before they could progress to higher levels of personal fulfillment?

---

84. A. Maslow, "A Theory of Human Motivation," *Psychological Review*. 1943, 50, 370–96.

1. Physical requirements for survival including air, water, food, clothing, and shelter
2. Personal requirements for safety and security including physical and financial security and health
3. Good friendships and loving relationships
4. Competence fostered by independence, self-confidence, and freedom

With these needs satisfied, Maslow believed human beings would then pursue two higher level needs:

1. Self-actualization, or realizing their full potential by becoming the very best person they could be at whatever they chose to do
2. Self-transcendence, or pursuing higher goals beyond themselves such as helping others develop to their full potential and investing their energies to improve the condition of mankind

Research appears to validate the existence of these universal needs, even though it hasn't supported the hierarchical theory of how they play out[85]. Nonetheless, Maslow's theory remains one of the most popular in psychology.

From a practical standpoint, it basically means that people can't achieve self-fulfillment or self-actualization, much less self-transcendence, while actively devoting the bulk of their energies to life demands such as succeeding in school and career, skillfully parenting and raising children, or fighting disease and chronic illness.

It's a given that when your basic needs are threatened, meeting them takes precedence over pursuing higher order needs. A soldier fighting for his life focuses on safety and security. A person going through a trying divorce or the death of a child focuses on how to survive these painful experiences.

---

85. Saul MacLeod, "Maslow's Hierarchy of Needs," *Simply Psychology*, 2017, http://www.simplypsychology.org/maslow.html.

People struggling with poor self-esteem or mastering a difficult job focus on addressing these challenges. In other words, when you experience a threat, you don't have the luxury of pursuing higher order needs that can result in great self-fulfillment.

But once basic needs are met, self-fulfillment becomes possible. Even busy individuals can devote time to self-improvement and learning. Going to the gym, reading great works, and visiting wonderful museums are just a few examples of how people enrich their lives. Reading this book and considering the wisdoms it presents is another example.

Some of the busy leaders I counseled at the very top of huge organizations managed to pursue hobbies or charitable causes, yet while many felt fulfilled, few of them had enough energy left to pursue self-actualization. To be fully self-actualized, you have to become the architect of your own unique goals. You have to realize a greater appreciation of your life, make new discoveries about yourself, and pursue peak experiences you have never encountered before... and I don't mean from artificially induced drug highs!

What is self-actualization? Picture yourself at a crossroads in life. Having achieved recognition and financial security, you now want more. The actualization road lies ahead of you, and it must be your own uniquely designed creation. Only you can decide what will add value to your life. This endeavor will test your resourcefulness and maturity and will require great self-examination, which you might recall lies at the core of wisdom.

Psychologist Mihaly Csikszentmihalyi's study of experiences that lead to great personal fulfillment led him to identify "flow" experiences in which individuals report being totally absorbed and thriving[86]. Surprisingly, he discovered there's no one magic pursuit or formula for what Maslow called self-actualization. In fact, Csikszentmihalyi found that even people who aren't particularly well educated or well known can achieve the psychological state of total fulfillment or "flow."

---

86. Mihaly Csikszentmihalyi, *Flow: The Psychology of Optimal Experience*, New York: Harper and Row, 1990.

Csikszentmihalyi concluded that flow experiences occur when individuals make a great personal and psychological investment in what they are doing. Their efforts in turn compel them to discover what additional goals or activities they can accomplish.

I imagine Thomas Edison experienced this fully absorbed state while inventing the electric light bulb. If you're interested, watch the 1940 movie *Edison, the Man* starring Spencer Tracy. Watch how Edison uses resourcefulness and his great maturity to handle failure after failure searching for just the right filament to make light bulbs glow. This self-educated man filed over one thousand patents in his career. His lifetime of inventions must have been extraordinarily fulfilling!

Another example of achieving this state of flow involves a working man who was not at all famous[87]. A gardener for a small Italian company, he created and designed an exceptionally magnificent garden as well as his own unique gardening tools. The company and the public marveled at the beauty of his work, and he reported that he was most proud of his crossbred flowers blooming in various striking colors. This individual was most assuredly self-actualized. Had he gone on to write a world-class book on gardening for others to enjoy or one that influenced a new movement in horticulture, I believe Maslow would have characterized his life as transcendent. As it was, he experienced his job every day as a continuous flow experience.

Not all of us will reach self-actualization, but we can all experience "peak" moments. My first peak experience occurred when I was 40 years old. My career was successful and I was very busy, yet I was struggling with turning 40. How would the second half of my life turn out? Was I managing my career, or was it managing me? Did I have sufficient time for self-reflection and new learning? Was I growing as a person?

I decided to take a camping trip to the Arizona desert with some friends. We invited a Smithsonian Museum guide to plan our trip and introduce

---

[87]. Mihaly Csikszentmihalyi, *Flow: The Psychology of Optimal Experience*, New York: Harper and Row, 1990.

us to Native American folklore and desert living. However, what I wanted most was to wake up, leave camp early after breakfast, and hike aimlessly by myself all day in the high desert listening to my Louis Armstrong audiotape of great jazz. I followed through on this desire, and what a peak experience it was! The sun came up, the cold desert turned warm and inviting, and cacti bloomed all over the serene and beautiful landscape as I listened to Armstrong, fully one with myself and nature.

At that moment, it dawned on me that the second half of my life would play out well as long as I continued to learn and grow personally. This was wisdom striking me in a wonderfully pristine setting. I realized I didn't need answers for all my midlife questions. Just being able to clearly articulate the questions was enough for now. The answers would come in due time.

Now that I'm past 70, I can indeed answer those midlife questions. Funny how hindsight brings self-awareness. That's why it's so illuminating to pause and look back. As I replay my highs, I realize even more about myself. For example, many if not most of my high points came as I enjoyed myself in unspoiled natural settings. My peak experience in the desert was just the first of many. Here are a few other peak experiences I've enjoyed:

- Catching a 125-pound sailfish off the coast of Cabo San Lucas… What a fight!
- Jet skiing through the beautiful Greek islands and caves… Exhilarating!
- Helicoptering into the Grand Canyon and over the mouth of an active Hawaiian volcano… Awe-inspiring!
- Riding a dog sled on the top of a huge glacier mountain in Alaska… Breathtaking!
- Yachting along the magnificent Italian Amalfi coast and caves of Italy… Fantastic!

These peak experiences are all part of self-actualization because they form a pattern that greatly influences my joy. Looking back at these experiences helps me realize how I can design a path of happiness that enriches the rest of my life. Trips that lie ahead include seeing the Swiss Alps up close, snorkeling the Great Barrier Reef in Australia, and taking a cruise around the world.

In addition to self-actualization, I will also reach transcendence if I do something extraordinary to give back to the world. To clarify the difference between self-actualization and self-transcendence, read the two case studies below. Each is a composite of actual individuals I counseled in my practice.

Case # 1: *This individual lived a modest life as a child, then married into a successful commercial business. His wife ran the business and he ran the back office with great efficiency. The couple eventually divorced. The divorce was painful, but after many legal battles and repeated court appearances, he received one half of the assets of a profitable business. Exhausted and emotionally drained, he retired and moved to a city with many retirees that afforded excellent medical care, parks, a leading university with courses for seniors, and a great art community. He had just begun taking courses and meeting new people when he suffered a heart attack. He was sent to the university's cardiac care center, where a leading surgeon removed his heart clot. He recovered fully and began carefully following a prescribed program of exercise and diet. In the course of all this, he met many new cardiac friends, and he is just starting to go to museums and art fairs with some of them. He feels he has a second lease on life and is very grateful for his recovery. While he is beginning the journey to self-actualization, he is nowhere near achieving the emotional state of transcendence. Nonetheless, if he begins to volunteer his time (as his friends do already) at the cardiac center, it's possible he might be able to achieve transcendence. Much will depend on whether he becomes a volunteer and whether the experience leads to greater happiness, self-discovery, and a continued desire to be involved in improving the lives of others.*

Case # 2: *This individual acquired considerable wealth in a medical practice that she thoroughly enjoyed creating and growing. After retiring, she relocated to a beautiful seaside condominium and furnished it with the help of a well-known designer. She enjoys her life a great deal and is active, plays sports, and writes books. One of her novels recently made the <u>New York Times</u> best seller's list. Before publishing her first novel, she started a book club with a number of close friends, and their monthly meetings are a rich and stimulating* *part of her life. In fact, her friends urged her to pursue her dream of writing. She is close to her two adult children and is glad they live nearby and visit often. She just started a family foundation for charitable giving and is now beginning to reach out to community agencies, particularly the American Cancer Society. Her spouse died of cancer, and one of her children successfully beat breast cancer a few years ago. She is clearly self-actualized, and it doesn't take a psychologist to know she is well on her way to realizing a personal state of transcendence, too.*

I am also clearly self-actualized. I love nature, and as a result I live in a seaside tropical home with great water views. Florida sunsets are often brilliant orange and light the night sky in a myriad of colors. I'm treated to these extraordinary moments of visual beauty almost every day, and these experiences add much richness and fulfillment to my life. Still, self-actualization isn't the same as self-transcendence. According to Maslow, striving for goals beyond oneself is at the very top of the hierarchy of needs. I believe this is a journey that has no boundaries.

Take Bill Gates, America's richest person. He and his wife established a foundation that so far has given away 30 billion dollars in 14 years[88]. That huge fortune equals the worth of the top 20 people in America! The Bill & Melinda Gates Foundation is working to eliminate polio in three countries and to fight malaria and a host of other diseases that kill millions in underdeveloped countries. In the U.S., the foundation funds innovative education programs in city schools and community colleges, giving scholarships to talented students through the United Negro College Fund and funding joint ventures in technical education between schools and companies that hire graduates. This philanthropy is a great contribution to mankind, and no doubt the Gateses are finding these efforts do indeed transcend their own lives.

---

88. Kerry A. Dolan, "Like What the Gates Foundation Is Doing? Now You Can Donate to Its Efforts," *Forbes*, November 14, 2016, https://www.forbes.com/sites/kerryadolan/2016/11/14/like-what-the-gates-foundation-is-doing-now-you-can-donate-to-its-efforts/#58fbfda37636.

Barry M. Cohen, PhD

What about my efforts to achieve transcendence? For one thing, I'm working to improve the quality of the lives of young adults with lifelong degenerative disabilities. This effort began almost 10 years ago when my son asked me to write a book with him to help disabled students with all kinds of limitations prepare themselves for the transition from school to work and to cope with the many life challenges they will inevitably face.

My son has myotonic dystrophy, the same disease my wife died from. As a result, I've become immersed in the myotonic community of doctors, medical researchers, and families all over the country whose loved ones struggle with this disease. Last year, I lobbied congressmen in Washington, D.C., for the Myotonic Dystrophy Foundation, and our collective efforts led to the successful passage of an expanded Muscular Dystrophy Care Act.

For the past seven years, I've facilitated support groups for young adults with myotonic dystrophy. Among other efforts, I made a webinar giving advice for how to disclose this disease to other people who can make a big difference in their lives such as potential employers, educators, and romantic partners.

I never would have known of the myotonic dystrophy (MD) community had my loved ones not developed this disease, but their misfortune has led me to use my knowledge and resources to help those who are less fortunate than I am. I see this as a lifetime pursuit, and it's very fulfilling. As part of the myotonic dystrophy community, I've met people from all walks of life all over the United States I wouldn't otherwise have known. This work has made me a better person.

I also recently funded a 10-year national scholarship program for young adults to attend MD conferences where they can learn more about their disease and the latest medical advances. The funding is managed by a leading medical college and is administered by myotonic dystrophy families. Many young adults with MD and their families have formed lasting friendships while attending these conferences, which means these young people are no longer isolated from one another. Additionally, local state support groups are springing up all over the country. My son and I lead such a group in our state.

By mindfully using my experiences and resources to make other people's lives meaningful and rewarding, I'm well on my way to self-transcendence.

I'm also in the process of producing a webinar teaching people how to select the best possible caregivers for their disabled loved ones. This endeavor would put my psychological expertise to great use on behalf of others. If the webinar is successful and I donate the proceeds to the Myotonic Dystrophy Foundation, which seeks to cure the disease that took my wife's life and afflicts our son, my state of transcendence will soar!

Writing this book is another source of great fulfillment, self-actualization, and, yes, self-transcendence. I've written other books, but this one has been the most gratifying. I hope it helps bring wisdom to all who read it. Just remember, you have to discover your own life wisdoms in your own way. No one can copy anyone else's wisdoms; they can only learn from them.

I wrote this book at the request of my grandchildren, but I hope it will leave a lasting legacy for everyone seeking to realize their full life's potential. I hope my grandchildren are blessed with lives that are self-actualized and transcendent, and I hope every individual reading this book is similarly blessed. I know for certain some of you will be, both during and after my lifetime.

In sum, here are my wisdoms for self-fulfillment and beyond:

- Once basic needs are reasonably satisfied, we can afford to discover our full potential.

- To be the very best people we can be at whatever we choose to do is the equivalent of becoming fully self-actualized. It is a lifelong pursuit. To be fully self-actualized, we each have to become the architect of our own unique goals.

- Many very busy leaders at the top of organizations and even well-known accomplished people can be so immersed in their endeavors that they rarely have the energy left to pursue lives that are self-actualized.

- Examining your peak experiences during your lifetime can give you the wisdom to chart a course of great self-fulfillment later in life and well into retirement. Be your own architect for personal fulfillment.

- There is no magic formula for achieving personal fulfillment, but individuals from all walks of life and education do it. It is an extraordinary psychological state marked by total absorption in your accomplishments while maximally applying your talents, resources, and wisdoms.

- Some people not only reach a state of great personal fulfillment but also transcend their own accomplishments by giving back their talents, resources, and wisdoms for the greater good of mankind.

Recommended Readings

Internet References

Dolan, Kerry A. "Like What the Gates Foundation Is Doing? Now You Can Donate to Its Efforts." *Forbes*, November 14, 2016. https://www.forbes.com/sites/kerryadolan/2016/11/14/like-what-the-gates-foundation-is-doing-now-you-can-donate-to-its-efforts/#58fbfda37636.

MacLeod, Saul. "Maslow's Hierarchy of Needs." *Simply Psychology*, 2017. http://www.simplypsychology.org/maslow.html.

"Maslow's Hierarchy of Needs." *Wikipedia*, last modified April 6, 2018. https://en.wikipedia.org/wiki/Maslow%27s_hierarchy_of_needs, accessed April 9, 2018.

Print References

Csikszentmihalyi, Mihaly. *Flow: The Psychology of Optimal Experience*. New York: Harper and Row. 1990.

Maslow, A. "A Theory of Human Motivation." *Psychological Review*. 1943, 50, 370–96.

Inspiration

THE FOLLOWING QUOTES are from famous people from every walk of life. They are a testimony that accomplished people have great wisdom to share with all those taking life's journey. Together, we are all part of a great community called planet Earth.

"Life is an endless opportunity for growth. I had new insights about myself in the past six months. It's the most delicious surprise of surprises." ~ **Norman Lear**
"Knowledge speaks but wisdom listens." ~ **Jimi Hendrix**
"There is no path to happiness. Happiness is the path." ~ **Buddha**
"I've failed over and over and over again in my life, and that is why I succeed." ~ **Michael Jordan**
"I took a walk in the woods and came out taller than the trees." ~ **Henry Thoreau**
"The art of living is not controlling what happens to us but using what happens to us." ~ **Gloria Steinem**
"Life is like a movie. Write your own ending. Keep believing." ~ **Jim Henson**
"In the end, it's not the years in your life that count… It's the life in your years." ~ **Attributed to Abraham Lincoln, Adlai Stevenson, and others**

Finally, I want to share with you the rules of positive living offered by a great Eastern thought leader considered one of the wisest individuals to ever walk the planet, the fourteenth Dalai Lama:

Barry M. Cohen, PhD

18 Rules of Positive Living

1. Take into account that great love and great achievements involve great risk.
2. When you lose, don't lose the lesson.
3. Follow the three Rs: respect for self, respect for others, and responsibility for all your actions.
4. Remember that not getting what you want is sometimes a wonderful stroke of luck.
5. Learn the rules so you know how to break them properly.
6. Don't let a little dispute injure a great friendship.
7. When you realize you've made a mistake, take immediate steps to correct it.
8. Spend some time alone every day.
9. Open your arms to change, but don't let go of your values.
10. Remember that silence is sometimes the best answer.
11. Live a good, honorable life. Then when you get older and think back, you'll be able to enjoy it a second time.
12. A loving atmosphere in your home is the foundation for your life.
13. In disagreements with loved ones, deal only with the current situation. Don't bring up the past.
14. Share your knowledge. It's a way to achieve immortality.
15. Be gentle with the earth.
16. Once a year, go someplace you've never been before.

17. Remember that the best relationship is one in which your love for each other exceeds your need for each other.
18. Judge your success by what you had to give up in order to get it.

Afterword:
Wisdom Takeaways from Millennials

Dear Readers,

Wisdom comes from all kinds of personal experiences refined by our ability to draw meaning from them in order to understand and successfully manage our lives.

With that in mind, I invited four millennials to read several chapters in my book and then write "Dear Dr. Cohen letters" reflecting on the takeaways they received and any thoughts they have on the possible positive impact of these life skills going forward to further enrich their life's journeys.

Specifically, I invited a millennial who has experienced significant past trauma, a high school senior seeking to understand motivation and self-discipline, a parent who recently remarried and finds herself parenting five children (his and hers), including older millennial teens and kids in their early twenties, and an adult man with Asperger syndrome searching for a new job.

Why these particular individuals? I wanted a cross-section of millennials. Some have post-graduate degrees and some have no degree. Some are currently struggling with their lives and others are thriving. Some are working full time in chosen careers and others have part-time jobs or are still in school.

Consequently, the following letters reflect very different perspectives along life's journey. The great social psychologist Kurt Lewin advanced a theory of perception over 85 years ago. He said that all of us live in our own "life spaces" that include the totality of our behaviors and needs and the sum total of our wisdoms. (Read more about Dr. Lewin at http://web.sonoma.edu/users/d/daniels/lewinnotes.html.)

We all live in our own unique life spaces. The four "Dear Dr. Cohen" letters that follow will hopefully provide a window into the special life spaces of these millennials and perhaps whet your appetite to reread select chapters or reflect on those life skills that speak to you as you further navigate your own life's journeys.

May each of your lives be enriched with an abundance of wisdom.

Dr. Barry M. Cohen

Kira is a 27-year-old graduate of a leading university. She works in public health with a focus on HIV and AIDS. She grew up in a large urban city and is an only child to parents she describes as "the best." She loves beaches and gelato, and her friends mean the world to her. She recently lived in Costa Rica, where she learned fluent Spanish and volunteered in a local medical clinic. This fall, she begins graduate studies to become a physician assistant. Eventually, she hopes to work in family medicine and pediatrics. She focused on the chapters on resilience and happiness in her letter.

Dear Dr. Cohen,

Thank you so much for sharing your wisdoms in your newest book. Your chapters on resilience and happiness made me reflect on my experiences as a college freshman, when I developed severe ulcerative colitis and, for a time, struggled to be resilient or happy.

In spite of my best efforts and the help of my doctor, I became so sick that I was unable to attend class. I was very unhappy, and for a time, I lost hope. This was a big change for me. Until now, I had been one of the happiest people I'd ever met.

The severity of my illness resulted in three surgeries to remove my colon and create a j pouch. While many people with ulcerative colitis struggle to make the decision to undergo this procedure, I had no more options, so the right choice became clear very quickly. As soon as I woke up from the anesthesia from the first operation, I felt human again. That first surgery gave me back my hope. Sure enough, without the diseased organ, my body began to function again.

It took years to regain my physical strength and emotional confidence, but I finally felt optimistic about the future. I had learned a tough lesson about the relationship between resilience and happiness. In this world of ours, it seems almost impossible to be fully happy if you're not resilient.

Six years later, I am thrilled to report that I've never felt happier. I sometimes think about the trauma I experienced, but it feels like a lifetime ago. Even so, I must admit that my happiness didn't instantly return to me; I had to work on myself and practice lots of self-care.

When I think about my friends, I realize that most of them haven't suffered severe trauma, yet they still seem less happy than I am. Could it be that I have a special confidence that comes from knowing I can overcome any obstacle that comes my way? I don't let small challenges stress me the way they used to, and I'm extremely positive. Things do go wrong, but there is always a silver lining, and I like to challenge myself to find it. While I do not believe that everything happens for a reason, I like to turn each situation on its head to find the good. I am constantly reminded that life is short and that every day is a gift. I'm also not afraid to make my own decisions and travel off the beaten path. I know I must be true to myself and that my path will be unique.

Thanks to my illness, I've had the opportunity to consider what I most value, and I know I want to give back to people who need help. When I was in the hospital, I realized that if I were lucky enough to regain my strength, I wanted to dedicate my life to helping others regain theirs. To me, there is nothing more meaningful than working in health care. Helping others has become my calling.

As I look ahead, I'm excited to see more of the world, to experience new cultures, and to connect with people from all over. I plan to collect experiences, not money, and to cherish relationships, not possessions. I'm still discovering what excites and motivates me, and I will continue to listen to myself every step of the way.

Reading your book has helped me put some of my emotions into words and has validated many of my experiences. I will hold your words close to my heart as my adventure continues.

Kira

Lester is a 17-year-old high school student. A hard-working senior, he lives in a large suburban area with his parents and 13-year-old brother. The family is close, and Lester's dad has been his closest mentor. Lester played baseball throughout middle school and lacrosse in high school and enjoyed some success, though he wasn't a superstar. He is popular and has a number of friends; some have been a positive influence and some have not. He's also had a number of part-time jobs, including running a pressure-cleaning business. He has applied to a number of colleges and expects to be accepted by several. This coming summer, he is enrolled in an entrepreneurial program for promising high school students at a large business school in New York City. This will be his first taste of college.

Dear Dr. Cohen,

    I wanted to read your chapters on motivation and maturity because I'm having a tough time right now with my academic studies and also struggling a bit with friends. My motivation throughout high school has always gotten me where I want to be, but I've learned the hard way that the friends you hang out with are a huge part of what motivates you. In the past few years, I've had several close friends negatively impact my academic motivation. Eventually, I let these friends go, but it took a while. Through trial and error, I feel like I've learned what I need to keep me motivated and on the right path.

    A striking wisdom you mentioned was to never set a goal so high that you couldn't reach it but instead to set small specific goals. When I was in middle school, I was a serious baseball player. All my goals were high, and many of my coaches, including my father, were skeptical that they were attainable. Setting these goals motivated me to play well, and eventually I met my final goal. I was always taught to set high goals with the idea that if I didn't reach them, I'd still land so high that I wouldn't be disappointed. If I'd set smaller goals in baseball, I might have reached my end goal faster and been more in love with the game. Instead, I found baseball frustrating.

    I'm entering college soon, and one of my goals is to join a frat. When trying to become a member, you drink, party, and do a number of questionable things to try to convince other frat members to select you. I hope to cultivate the wisdom and discipline to ask myself probing questions before I make impulsive decisions based on my motivation. Partying is a huge part of college, and at high school parties, I'm slowly learning to ask myself why I'm doing something before it leads to danger.

Another great wisdom I hope to use is the knowledge of how motivating ups and downs can be. In school, I'm used to getting almost all "A"s. Whenever I make a mistake that might jeopardize my grade-point average, I have a panic attack. This wisdom helps me realize that something less than an "A" won't be fatal and that mistakes are natural and even motivating. I take almost all advanced and honors classes, and every year when I sign up, I think, "What if I fail?" This motivates me to work hard, and every year, signing up for hard classes turns out to be the right choice. The part I haven't quite mastered is the fear of failure. In the future, knowing I have a habit of meeting difficult goals might help me avoid so many panic attacks.

I've also been thinking a lot about your advice to take risks when the outcome depends on skill, not chance. In the past, I've made some stupid decisions that bit me right back because I relied on other people. For example, this year I took an advanced Spanish class knowing the only prayer I had of passing was being tutored by my friend. I took the class anyway because it would look good on my college application. My friend helped me for half the course but wound up not having enough time. In the future, I'm only going to take risks when I know the outcome depends on me, not on someone else doing something for me.

Thank you for your insights.

Lester

Reese just turned 40 years old. She married two years ago into a large family after being a single mom to two children now ages 14 and 19. Her three stepchildren are both older and younger than her own children. Reese is truly a millennial. She's also parenting multiple millennial kids along with maintaining a demanding full-time career. In her late twenties, she ran her own business, and today she is a senior designer and top salesperson in a family-owned kitchen and bathroom remodeling business where she supervises a staff of designers. In her free time, Reese loves visiting with family and friends, being outdoors, playing with her dog, and cooking. She cannot live without chips and salsa or books, which bring peace to her busy life. Reese chose to read the chapters on leadership and financial habits.

Dear Dr. Cohen,

At age 18, I began working in retail and was soon promoted to the position of supervisor. To my chagrin, I found that about half the employees who used to respect me suddenly began ignoring me. I could not understand this. I tried to put my feelings aside and manage everyone with an even hand, but some people joked that I "made people cry." I simply could not understand how I had developed the reputation of coming down hard on people just because I called them out when they made mistakes.

At the time, I thought emotions had little to do with business. When management decided to move me into a more "suitable" position, I thought this was unfair, but eventually I came to realize that this was one of the best learning experiences I ever had. I now realize that I didn't really fail. Rather, I learned I was very unprepared to lead others. I needed to mature as a person and to learn the art of leadership.

This experience taught me a lot. I now realize that accomplished leaders must motivate others to succeed. There are many ways to unlock the energy of subordinates. Some people need a lot of strokes; others need very few. Trust has to be earned, and respect requires communicating with and listening to others. Above all, leaders must be models of maturity. If I'd had a great leadership coach, my first experience as a supervisor might have turned out differently!

As the years went by, I found myself self-employed with various companies that trusted me to work with little to no supervision. At one point, I made a deal with a company: if I reached or exceeded our agreed-upon sales goal in six months, I would be given 48% of the business. I reached the goal in three months! The business grew quickly, and soon I was leading installers, salespeople, and my office manager. I was only 28, and soon I was struggling to balance my life as a single adult with a busy job. Looking back, I just wanted to hang out with my friends. I did not keep an eye on the changing market, and in the fallout of the recession of 2008, I lost my business.

I realize today that leadership is as much about growing and maturing personally as it is about learning specific skills. For example, all leaders need to learn the art of delegation. They have to learn how to be flexible and to determine how much latitude to give others. Some workers need close supervision, but most people enjoy autonomy and the freedom to decide how to accomplish their goals. In other words, managers have to learn how to get the best out of their employees. Leadership can indeed be learned, and leaders improve as they acquire experience, learn from accomplished mentors, and figure out how to do things better and better.

Needless to say, leadership is incredibly complex. Some things I do well naturally. Some things I've learned from failure. And some things I've learned from people around me who are talented in their own right. As you said, Dr. Cohen, leadership is a process, and this brings me to where I am today.

I was promoted to my current leadership position after my boss left the company. He was a skilled communicator, but he struggled to be a good leader. The problem was, he didn't understand how to lead. He wanted to motivate us, but he had no idea how to recognize our talents or get the best out of us. I agreed to take over his job not because I wanted the position but because the people I worked with had no one to lead them.

I am far more flexible and trusting of the people who work for me than he was. Even those who aren't directly under my supervision have begun coming to me for advice. I was recently put in charge of training and developing new salespeople, and I'm a mentor as well. The list of my responsibilities keeps growing, and I'm also growing personally, too. For example, my leadership skills are helping me be more effective at home. I am very demanding of myself, even more demanding than others are of me. I don't want power, but I do enjoy earning respect. I clearly have a high need for achievement.

I was excited to read your chapter called "Savvy Financial Habits," too. I have always been a smart shopper. I buy great products but only on sale or after bargaining for them. I prefer to cook at home rather than eat out. When we first got married, I showed my husband that he was spending at least $70.00 a week on fast food but complaining that he couldn't pay off debt. I told him to use the $70 per week toward one balance at a time, and he ended up paying off his debt in one year!

Your chapter gave me many ideas on how to plan my financial goals and form better saving and investment habits. Your words "Your salary isn't enough" really struck me. I'm making substantially more money than ever before, but my husband and I only recently started IRA accounts. I wish I'd known some of these tips in my twenties or even two years ago. I had good saving habits, but I knew very little about investing.

I'm now shopping around for mortgages and have decided to look for a property with a small cottage or guesthouse if it's affordable. I also want to look into passive investments. I can tell I need to invest more and let time do the work.

Living within my means and not taking what I have for granted has always been a reality for me. I've tried my best to show my kids how much it takes to earn a dollar and save. I want to learn as much as possible about investing and to teach them to start early!

Thanks for helping make me ever wiser!

Reese

Barry M. Cohen, PhD

Josh is a 28-year-old high school graduate who is challenged with Asperger syndrome. For the past nine years, he has been a vet assistant for a busy veterinary practice. He enjoys serving customers and helping to care for their pets, and he particularly likes helping elderly pet owners. He lifts their sick animals for them and even transports their pets to the clinic when needed. In his spare time, he enjoys hanging out with friends, playing cards, and just having fun. He is dating someone special now, and he can see the relationship growing fairly serious soon. He loves his job, but he has a new boss, and some challenges have arisen. He read the chapter on resourcefulness, and it clearly made an impact on him.

Dear Dr. Cohen,

I'm in a bind. I worked for a wonderful veterinarian for nine years, helping her care for many of my hometown's pet population. She recently retired and sold her practice to a new doctor. My new boss is not so stellar. Under this new vet, I have had my hours drastically cut, and it's impacting my life a lot more than I thought it would. My paychecks are getting smaller but my bills certainly aren't. I've been waffling over whether to stay or go, but I know it's time to jump ship and join a better boat's crew. With my experience, it ought to be a cinch, but the roiling ocean that awaits me is terrifying.

One of my biggest hurdles is my mental condition. As an adult suffering from Asperger syndrome, I find it difficult to meet and connect with new people. It's very daunting to leave my comfort zone and seek new employment. Even more daunting is the fact that my last job hunt was almost a decade ago. It's been so long since I've had to look for work that I find myself alarmingly unprepared for this ordeal.

For starters, I need to put together a proper resume. Luckily, my mental condition opens doors to assistance. Once I have my resume in hand, I need to put myself out there, find someone who needs help, and introduce myself. I have to tell them about my syndrome and my desire to work for a vet of my former boss's caliber. The hardest part for me will be making the right impact during an interview once I land one. If I crash and burn in one interview, I have to keep positive and remember to use the experience gleaned for the next one. If all else fails, I have to fake it till I make it.

As a challenged millennial, if ever there was a need for a resourceful solution to my problem, now's the time to discover it. I have the right experience, and my former employer could help me. I need a game plan to find the right vet office that can use my skills. I don't want to leave my town or work in a different field. I think I need to "scout" some vet offices by calling local vets and asking about possible openings. I think I will mention my vet by name and explain that she recently retired. I also think I should phone her before going any further. She might even know some local vets she can recommend. If she can help me, my search might be incredibly easy. That could be a resourceful solution to "get my foot in the door"!

Finding the right coach to help me practice interviewing is important, too. This could help me land a position and also teach me better ways to communicate and meet my Asperger challenges! These skills might even help me to be a better communicator all my life. I have a general idea of what I need to do and an inkling of a plan, but it definitely needs some polish. Would you be willing to help me out with some mock interviews to help me prepare for the real deal? Now that's thinking outside the box!

Thanks in advance,

Josh

Barry M. Cohen, PhD

Appendix
Select Author Publications

Cohen, B. "Assessing and Developing High Potential Executives." *ASTD Dialog*. Fall 1990, 1–3.

Cohen, B. "Career Planning and Development, Specimen Checklist." *Personnel and Human Resources Administration*. Megginson, L. C. Richard Irwin Press. Homewood, IL. 1976.

Cohen, B. "Coping Skills Make All the Difference for Myotonic Dystrophy Families." *Reaching Out*. Fall, 1994.

Cohen, B. "Parenting Special Needs Teens in Crisis." *About Families*. July 2006, 15.

Cohen, B. & Etheredge, J. "Recruiting's Main Ingredient." *Journal of College Placement*. 1975, 35, 75–77.

Cohen, B. & Jaffee, C. L. "Assessment Centers in Government Agencies." *The Government Executive*. 1976, 4, 18–23.

Cohen, T. & Cohen, B. *Disabled & Challenged: Reach for Your Dreams!* WishingUwell Publishing: Clearwater, FL. 2005.

Cohen, T. & Cohen, B. *Travel Near & Travel Far: Step Out of Your Disabled World!* WishingUwell Publishing: Clearwater, FL. 2016.

R. K. Ready, J. M. Bernal, & Cohen, B. *Organizational Behavior: A Learning by Doing Approach*. University of West Florida Press. 1977.

Select Author Presentations and Interviews

Cohen, B. "Assessments As a Change Strategy in a Global Company." Applied Psychology Congress. Mexico City, Mexico, 2000.

Cohen, B. "Developmental Applications of Assessment Technology." Center for Creative Leadership, Greensboro, N.C., 1986.

Cohen, B. "Disclosing & Talking about Your Disorder." *Myotonic Dystrophy Foundation.* http://www.myotonic.org/disclosing-talking-about-your-disorder.

Cohen, B. & Grissom, M. "Commitment to Development for Strategic Leaders." International Congress of Organization Development. Monterrey, Mexico, 1995.

Glusac, Elaine. "For the Disabled Traveler, Strategies for a Successful Trip." *New York Times*, February 3, 2017. https://www.nytimes.com/2017/02/03/travel/disabled-traveler-strategies-for-a-successful-trip.html?mwrsm=Email.

"Top 4 Things to Think about When Traveling with a Disability." *Christopher & Dana Reeve Foundation,* April 7, 2017. https://www.christopherreeve.org/blog/daily-dose/top-4-things-to-think-about-when-traveling-with-a-disability.

Barry M. Cohen, PhD

About the Author

Dr. Barry M. Cohen began graduate studies in 1965 at Columbia University in vocational psychology, career assessment, and counseling. After graduating, he received a non-service fellowship to attend the University of Tennessee's newly formed Industrial Organizational Psychology Doctoral Program. There, Dr. Cohen gained firsthand exposure to programs in leadership assessment, team building, and organizational behavior. He completed his doctoral dissertation in organizational leadership at Oak Ridge National Laboratories and the Tennessee Valley Authority.

Dr. Cohen was licensed in Florida as a psychologist in 1969. He did post-doctoral studies at Harvard University in executive coaching and Boston University in clinical assessment in 1976. That same year, he was a visiting scholar and professor at the MIT Sloan School of Management.

Dr. Cohen served as a member of the faculty of the University of West Florida from 1969–1978. He held joint appointments in psychology and management and developed its graduate program in industrial-organizational psychology. He also designed and taught the university's first career and life planning seminar for undergraduates seeking career-planning guidance.

In 1969, Dr. Cohen began his own firm, which grew into a nationally recognized leader in executive assessment, development of high-potential managers, and coaching. Global companies retained the firm including such leaders in industry as United Technologies, Oppenheimer, American Express, Pepsi, Phillip Morris, Pacific Gas & Electric, and Aetna Corporation. Government agencies included the U.S. Navy, the Department of the Interior, and the Small Business Administration.

After Dr. Cohen's retirement, he continued his professional work with young adults with disabilities and co-wrote two books with his son, who has myotonic dystrophy. Dr. Cohen presents workshops for millennials at the national conferences for the Myotonic Dystrophy Foundation headquartered in San Francisco. He also serves on the professional advisory council of Homebound Resources. Dr. Cohen is currently preparing a webinar on selecting high-quality caregivers for the Myotonic Dystrophy Foundation. He eventually hopes to offer this webinar to families with disabled family members across the United States and Canada.

www.ingramcontent.com/pod-product-compliance
Lightning Source LLC
Chambersburg PA
CBHW070055080526
44586CB00013B/1067